Orange Moments

How My Worst Nightmare Opened My Eyes and Allowed Me to Witness Hope

Laura Schupbach

ISBN 978-1-64416-580-5 (paperback)
ISBN 978-1-64458-496-5 (hardcover)
ISBN 978-1-64416-581-2 (digital)

Christian Faith Publishing, Inc.
832 Park Avenue
Meadville, PA 16335
www.christianfaithpublishing.com

Printed in the United States of America

For Wyatt, Tristan, and Colton.
Thank you for being my blessings.
Hugs, Kisses, High fives.

Contents

Foreword

When you think of a super woman, a heroine of strength and purpose, you immediately think of Super Woman. She can fight the toughest battles and the meanest foes, never messing up her hairdo or wrinkling her cape. And let's remember, Super Woman is now a senior citizen with unfading beauty who can still fly through the air with the greatest of speed, power and strength... all without belly fat or crow's feet.

My super woman is Laura Schupbach. She is dynamic, vibrant and on point for what God has called her to do. She is a woman who has risen like a phoenix from the ashes to be a "So That" woman! (2 Corinthians 1:3-4). In her book "Orange Moments", Laura has gifted you with a window into her grief, loss and sorrow. It's a tragedy that no parent would choose; but as a Christ Follower, she has trusted God for a purpose greater than her pain. She is a heroine of the faith!

As far as I know, Laura doesn't wear a cape or fly through the air, but she has allowed the Lord to clothe her in His righteousness and empower her, through the Holy Spirit, to overcome the destructive foes of depression, guilt and anger... even at God. There hasn't ever been a sympathy card created that could minister enough healing words to mend the broken heart of a grieving parent who has lost a child. It is only God's Word that can set you free!

On December 16, 2017 my husband and I celebrated our 50th wedding anniversary. As founders of our 25-year-old ministry, we were blessed to have many friends, family members and "sons" and "daughters" of our ministry present to celebrate this momentous event. As Laura's spiritual mom, mentor, and Bible teacher, she wrote the following words to me: "Thank you for another beautiful day. Being around all of you is like medicine for my emotions. It brings that kind of peace that surpasses all understanding. I should be upset. I should be crying. I should be miserable but here I am smiling. That's peace that only comes from God. I cry every day; but on this day, I caught myself smiling and even laughing at times. Thank you for that and for the very special way you chose to 'Pay it forward' with a scholarship in memory of Tristan. It is no coincidence the next retreat for this ministry is "Anchor of Hope". For the last two years of his life, Tristan wore a shirt that said, "Hope More Than Meets the Eye". I miss him so very much. Every day is a struggle, but I struggle a little less now as I have chosen to seek God for His purpose in my pain."

Everyone on earth has pain. It could be physical pain, financial pain, vocational pain, or pain in a relationship. The healing is in asking God to give you a purpose bigger than your pain. Laura Schupbach has done that in "Orange Moments". John 8:32 says, "You shall know the truth and the truth shall set you free." The truth is not facts or any self-help book. The Truth is a person... The Lord Jesus Christ. Laura has allowed the Truth to bring healing to her broken heart. As you allow this truth-filled book to minister to the deepest part of your soul, my prayer for you... and I know Laura well enough to know that she would concur... May the Truth set you free. It's not instant like ordering a Happy Meal and expecting it at the next window. It's day by day. Sometimes it's hour by hour or even moment by moment... ORANGE MOMENTS!

Mary Lucy Holliday, MA, C.I.S.D.
Founder and Executive Director
Sonflower Ministries
www.sonflower.com

Acknowledgments

Special thanks to family and friends for the support; to amazing neighbors, our church community, school parents and staff for countless prayers, meals, and ongoing thoughtfulness; and to our employers for their flexibility and tremendous loyalty. Our family is forever indebted to all of you.

Shout out to Heather for getting me out of the house time and time again when I didn't want to. "I'll go, I'll go, I'll go." *Exercise relieves stress and brings clarity.*

To sweet Eleanor, my prayer warrior, thank you for our Wednesday afternoons.

To all the moms I've met in the same boat as me, may God continue to comfort our broken hearts.

Introduction

I always described faith to my boys as believing without seeing and knowing something is true even if others say it isn't. Faith is having hope when all else is lost. If I'd heard or read someone's account of having their faith tested, it meant despite what happened, no matter how terrible, they still believed in God and in His will. I describe faith as trust in God no matter the circumstances. I've had a belief in God all my life. If your faith has never been tested, I believe it's not a matter of *if*—it's *when*. Listening to an online sermon one day, the pastor said, "It's not an easier path we need. It's stronger shoes." *I love that.* Size 7½, please.

For years, I've said "everyone has a story" in an attempt to be mindful of others in a world where it is so easy to get caught up in our own lives, and when something big happens, well, we want the world to stop. I know my world didn't stop at times when others came to a screeching halt. We hear "you are not alone" because we all know you're not the only one going through whatever it is you're going through. You know your family, friends, coworkers, neighbors, acquaintances, and even strangers have all gone through *something*, and chances are, there is at least one person on the face of this earth that has gone through the *same* thing. Often, we don't have the time to recognize someone else's story because either they didn't feel comfortable sharing it or we never even had the chance to meet. *So many people, so many stories.*

Have you ever been in line at the grocery store and wondered about the life of the person in front of you? I might see someone standing there waiting for the cashier with a look of despair. I would wonder, what is their story? Are they just having a moment, or is it something more? Are they having a bad day, a situation at home or work that has them preoccupied, or has something changed them forever? Are they struggling with a relationship or struggling financially? I'd stop and say a little prayer: "Lord, help this person with whatever is on their mind." Aren't we all struggling? Everyone has a story. Everyone has a cross they are carrying; some are just heavier than others. I felt as if I'd been given the heaviest cross of all.

I was always friendly with the cashiers at the grocery store. They'd ask how I was doing; I'd say, "Great. How is your day?" with a beaming smile. After Tristan died, I was the one in line with the look of despair. My answer changed from "great" to "I'm doing all right." I couldn't even hide it from the grocery store clerk.

When we pray as a family before meals, we say, "Bless us, O' Lord, and these, thy gifts, which we are about to receive from thy bounty through Christ our Lord, *and make us ever mindful of the needs of others.* Amen." The last part is an add-on my husband's grandparents put in years ago, and I think they'd be happy to hear us all still saying it that way. I've always loved it: "make us mindful of the needs of others." Being mindful of the needs of others helped us see how blessed we are. Being mindful of others who do not have enough food makes us thankful we are only a drive-through away from our next meal! Being mindful makes us thankful for our warm beds, hot showers, and clean water as we know there are so many who do not live with these luxuries. Being mindful reminds us to be ready to care for others when they are in a time of need. It's not *if*—it's when.

We went from praying for others to having others pray for us. We were the "others." When people talk about awful situations, they think of it as something that happens to *other* people. This can't be happening to *us!* Maybe you're reading this because it happened. You're there right now, in the middle of a mess or a disaster, a crisis or a loss of utter disbelief. You can't ever go back to the way things were. For us, it was a perfect Sunday afternoon that turned into our worst nightmare.

Can we ever truly be prepared when the rug gets pulled out from under our feet? No, I don't think so. However, I was more spiritually prepared for what happened to us than I would have been had something like this come around fifteen or twenty years ago. I'm not saying everyone will go through what we've been through, but you've heard the saying "death and taxes," right? So you know you will eventually lose *someone* you love.

We expect to lose our grandparents and then our parents. There is a natural order, and in expecting it that way, we can accept it when it does happen. I've watched friends lose their parents at a young age, and even though we expect them to go before us, I've seen how difficult it is when they do go. Even if they were sick and you knew it was coming, it doesn't matter. It still hurts to lose someone you love.

When an eighty- or ninety-year-old person dies, we tend to say, "They've had a good long life." When the person is only in their sixties or seventies, we say, "It was too soon." We have this expectation that we are all destined to live into our eighties and nineties. When someone is under the age of sixty, it is certainly a shock, and when it's a child, unacceptable. So the obvious question is, "Why does God allow this kind of suffering?"

I've had my own losses and grief and have seen how others have suffered through relationship turmoil, abuse, neglect, and addiction. Suffering hurts no matter what form it comes in, and I've realized the grief I am shackled with is not much different than being shackled with an addiction. Suffering hurts no matter what form it comes in.

The director of our religious education program recently asked all the parents what our favorite story of the Old Testament was. We each provided input, recalling stories we'd heard since we were children and then I realized the common thread: each story we told spoke of trial and triumph, survival when the odds were against them. The ones we all loved were the ones where they never gave up hope.

The answer I have come to for the question "Why does God allow suffering?" is this: there is either a lesson to be learned or a purpose to fulfill. God created us to love Him. He gave us free will so we could *choose* to love Him. If we were created without the ability to choose, it wouldn't really be love. With free will, we have the opportunity to glorify Him with our thoughts, words, and actions. We do not have the benefit of knowing the future. Having lived more than forty years, I have experiences I pull from. Having received a bad grade on a test and then going back to study more and do better on the *next* test, you not only bump up your grade but also gain wisdom. Study hard, get good grades.

How many times have you used the phrase "if only I knew then what I know now"? I look at each trial as an opportunity to either learn something God is trying to reveal or fulfill a purpose He feels I'm capable of. Believe me, I'd be lying if I said I don't still ask God, almost daily, "*Why*, Lord? Why Tristan? Why did you let this happen? What do you want from me?"

I have a story of my own to tell and a message to convey; one I'm hoping will open your eyes as this experience has opened mine. As a parent, it was unimaginable. If you are experiencing similar circumstances or just grief in general, I'll say my marriage, my faith, and the support from family and friends are reasons why I'm still standing. The most important factor for our survival has been our *faith*. Faith is not just about believing in God; faith offers hope. My faith has given me hope that I will survive this, there is a reason, and I will see my son again.

If you do not currently have a faith foundation or have stepped away from a relationship with God, my hope is you find your way to Him after you've read my story. Everybody has a story; something in their past that has affected who they are today. Maybe you can relate to my story, or maybe I'll be a benchmark story—one you'll think back on when you're thankful for your blessings.

Our story felt like everyone else's benchmark for using the phrase "it could be worse." We felt we were given a prison sentence without committing a crime. There was no loss, no divorce, no money issue or problem at work that could trump our story. Well, there *are* worse things, but when you are in the dark, it's difficult to see anything but the pain.

My story created a path, allowing us to look at life through a different lens. It's as if a veil had been lifted, and I realized I'd been standing behind a curtain all this time. It's not the life I planned. We continue to say, "It wasn't supposed to be like this." Of course, *our* plan says it wasn't supposed to be like this. No one in their right mind would *ever* plan for this kind of pain. No, our plan was to watch our boys excel in school and sports. Our plan was to watch them grow closer to one another and then go off to college. Our plan was they would be each other's best man when they fell in love and decided to get married. Our plan was to spend birthdays and holidays with their wives and our grandchildren. Our plan was *we* would go first.

I've asked why a million times, and I've said, "It's not fair," even more yet I accept God's will. I continue to hear, "Trust Me, Laura," and I am waiting for the day the Lord says, "See, I told you it was going to be all right." Every day I wake up, it's still the first thing I think about. It's also the last thing I think about before I go to bed: *This is not my life. Wake up. Take me back.*

Background

Hi, I'm Laura. Pretty basic intro when meeting someone new, right? And then the questions come as we get to know one another. Next thing everyone asks: "You married? Kids?"

I respond, "Married, yes."

Kids. *There's that question.* How do I answer this one now?

My answer for several years was, "I have two boys." Now I have to pause and ask myself, do I go there? Do I just tell them I have one when in my heart, I will always have two? Do I say I have one son *and* an eleven-year-old in heaven? We pick and choose how we answer that question now. Some days, I'm like, "I am just not going there today." Other days, I dump things onto a poor stranger in my local coffee shop. I love meeting new people, but I hate that small talk is not so small anymore.

I was the firstborn in my family (aka "the perfect child"). My parents actually met on a blind date. My dad was in the Air Force, stationed in Indiana. He and his roommate rode the train to Chicago to see his roommate's girlfriend, and… she had a friend. My parents dated, got engaged, called it off, then *rescheduled* the wedding. Doh! Reprint the invitations!

My grandfather on my dad's side was a New York City police officer, and it was my dad's plan to move back to Manhattan and become a cop. My mom went from growing up in Omaha to living in Manhattan—quite a culture shock. They moved into a teeny-tiny apartment a block from my grandparents. How 'bout *that* for culture shock. Move to NYC, oh, and "we're going to live a block from my parents!" Once pregnant and about to add a crib into their living space, they moved into a larger apartment in the Bronx.

Fast forward to 1975 in NYC, and hundreds of police and firefighters were laid off. From July 1975 until November 1979, no police officers were hired or trained in the city of New York. Out of work, my parents moved back to the Midwest and got an apartment in a suburb of Chicago, minutes from where my maternal grandparents lived. My dad was hired onto a local police force where he remained for seventeen years.

Once my sister arrived, two kids in a two-bedroom apartment was getting cramped, so my parents bought a house where we stayed until my sister and I grew up and moved out on our own. Just two years after buying the home, my parents separated. I was ten years old. The separation lasted six years. *Yes, six years.* My dad moved home twice during that time, but he worked midnights, sleeping during most of the day, so some of my memories of him being at the house are fuzzy. I couldn't tell you whether my dad was there because he was visiting or because he was *living* there. When I was sixteen, they got divorced. Spending every other weekend at my dad's had become the norm. As a kid, I didn't mind going to my dad's for the weekend because he would do special things with us like take us to a museum or to the movies.

My mom did all the day-to-day stuff: cooking, cleaning, helping with homework, laundry, and managing the house. She became the mom *and* the dad, doing all the traditional mom things *plus* having to be the one to fix a broken toilet, mow the lawn, and keep us safe. She did not have it easy. She went back to work shortly after the separation to help make ends meet. She spent the majority of her career as an administrative assistant to the principal at a nearby high school and worked longer hours once I was old enough to babysit my sister.

I remember the first time I had to come home from school with my sister to let us into the house with the key I'd worn as a necklace around my neck. Being that my sister and I were five and a half years apart in age, babysitting was a regular thing. I'd spend time encouraging my sister to clean up her room or at least make a path to her bed (literally, the floor was covered with toys). Sometimes I'd do her hair. Other times, we played superwoman, and she'd "fly" on my feet, or we'd just play outside. My sister and I are BFFs, and we can laugh harder than any other friend I have. I'll never forget the first time she called me at college and asked for advice about a junior-high dilemma she was facing. From that point forward, the relationship flourished. *Babysitter turned best friend.*

The move to our house happened just after I'd started second grade at a new school. I'd gone from a public school to a Catholic school and stayed there through eighth grade, then attended a public high school. Let me just say, for the record, I hated high school. I *loathed* freshman and sophomore year. Girls were just mean, and I had the whole separation thing going on with my parents. You couldn't pay me a million dollars to redo high school. I have such empathy for my friends with girls in junior high and high school now. Social media makes it ten times harder.

From seventh grade through my freshman year in high school, I attended faith-based counseling designated for kids of separated or divorced families (Rainbows program). In seventh grade, there were only two of us. By eighth grade, there were six of us, and when I was a freshman, the group was easily double that. I went from being one of only two in my class in this situation to it being a normal thing to have separated or divorced parents. Every other weekend with my dad became a little problematic for me when I was in high school because top priority was spending time with my friends. My dad was still working midnights, so I can remember getting to his apartment and he'd have to sleep. I'd clean his apartment out of boredom. I was gearing up for graduation and independence soon to be achieved at college where my weekends would be mine.

On one of the last weekends before I had to go away to college, my dad picked us up to take us for the weekend. We were only a few blocks away, and he told us he got married. "What?" I said. "To *who?*" We didn't realize his "friend" was more than a friend, and they eloped and got married without telling us. I made my dad turn the car around. We had met her and spent time with her but had no idea there was a relationship. That's just the age, and I was naïve. A few months later, they were pregnant.

When my dad told me, I remember thinking, "Ick, you're forty-three!"—*ancient* to a seventeen-year-old. My new stepmom was only fifteen years older than me. Fifteen years is not that wide an age gap, so to me, she felt more like an aunt. She was nice and passionate about animals. She was close with her family, and I knew she tried hard to build a relationship with us. She knew how to sew and had made teddy bears for me and my sister with outfits to match our school colors. We'd picked out patterns, and she was going to teach us to sew our own clothes. Sewing—there's a skill many women my age did *not* learn. For the record, I *have* a sewing machine. I made *one* set of curtains to hang in Tristan's room before he was born. *I'll take my gold star now.*

My stepmom's learn-to-sew project was put to the side, and my little brother was born on their one-year wedding anniversary. Two weeks, later the unthinkable happened.

First Exposure

Growing up, we spent a lot of time with my grandparents, aunts, uncles, and cousins on my mom's side. We got together to celebrate birthdays and holidays, and summer pool parties were the norm at my aunt and uncle's house nearby. We all lived within about thirty minutes of each other, so getting together was easy. My grandparents eventually moved out of their house into an apartment, and the family got together at their place frequently so they didn't have to travel.

My grandmother developed breast cancer when she was only forty-seven and fought it for thirteen years as it traveled through her body, even *after* a double mastectomy. She died at only sixty years old. I adored my grandmother, and I am sure I would have had a wonderful relationship with her as an adult had I had the opportunity. I remember visiting her in the hospital a few times and then, that night, seeing my mom crying in the kitchen after receiving the call she was gone. At ten years old, I vividly remember going to her wake and the funeral. That was my first exposure to dealing with grief and, more importantly, watching how others coped with grief.

Fast forward to my senior year of high school, my stepmom had a known heart condition. She got pregnant a few months after she and my dad were married. They wanted to make sure there wouldn't be any complications. The doctor assured them they would be fine. My brother arrived two weeks premature, which isn't all that unusual. My dad was originally scheduled to attend an overnight orientation with me three hours away at college.

When my stepmom went into labor two weeks early, he had no choice but to drop me off and promise to be back in the morning. He drove three hours to drop me off and raced back to the hospital to drive another three hours to pick me up and three hours back again. Twelve hours in the car over two days in the midst of your wife having a baby. Perfect timing! I was terrified spending the next twenty-four hours solo even though in a few short months, I'd be on my own as a freshman anyway. It was more about being one of only two who attended the orientation *without* parents. The girl I was paired up with to spend the night in the dorms already knew people on campus, so she took off to meet them. I went to bed alone. She came back in the wee hours of the night. I couldn't wait for my dad to come back and pick me up.

When my dad arrived, he told me I had a new baby brother. We drove straight to the hospital. That would be the last time I saw my stepmom. I eventually went home. She and my dad brought my brother home from the hospital. Shortly thereafter, she went *back* into the hospital. She knew something was wrong. My dad told her, "You just had a baby. You're just tired"; it was more than that. I went back to my dad's to help take care of my newborn brother while she was in the hospital. I'd just turned eighteen, and already, I was getting a taste of what it was like to be a new mother: up all night, sleeping whenever the baby slept, doing laundry, making bottles.

The doctors explained the valve in my stepmom's heart was "stuck open." They had to bring her blood pressure way down to close the valve and then bring her blood pressure back up to normal. It was the middle of the night when we got the call that she had died. My brother was only two weeks old. It was unbelievable. My dad was a wreck. I couldn't comprehend how my dad, a cop working midnights, was going to take care of a baby? I was going off to college in the fall! Thankfully, her parents, my dad's new in-laws, lived above them in a two-flat, so they took on parental responsibilities for my brother during the day. Grandparents turned parents overnight. For the next several years, they helped raise my brother. They were so very sweet, and I took to them like my *own* grandparents for a while as I'd visit my brother when I was home from college. I so enjoyed the time spent with them.

Someone's decision to attempt to save my stepmom failed, and at only thirty-three years old, with a two-week-old baby at home, one year into a new marriage, she was gone.

I don't know what I thought when I was ten and my mom explained Grandma had gone to heaven. I could never really picture heaven. I knew it wasn't *here*, of this earth. I knew Grandma was with God. I pictured her young and vibrant again, no longer sick and certainly no need for a walker in heaven. Although I was sad when my grandmother passed, it wasn't emotionally draining for me. I watched my mom go through the grief of losing a parent, but it didn't consume me—at least, my ten-year-old mind wasn't consumed. Oh, to have the resiliency of being a child.

Watching my dad lose a wife with a newborn, that was more consuming, but again, I was somewhat removed. I didn't live with my dad, and months later, I left for college. I had only known my stepmom for less than two years. It still had an impact on my life. To me, it said accidents happen, and you don't always get to live out the life you planned. I lost my other three grandparents years following this incident. The expectation of losing them helped prepare us, but knowing it's coming doesn't always make it any easier. If you've loved deeply, you grieve deeply.

At a time when I *should* have continued to go to church to find answers for the circumstances surrounding my stepmom's death, I was only going on weekends when I was home from school. I think I went to the Newman Center on campus two or three times. I was distraught, knowing my brother would grow up never knowing his mother. I knew firsthand the level of involvement my dad had in *my* life, and I thought, would it be different for my brother? Although I had pressing questions about life and what happens after, I was more focused on friends, my boyfriend, college classes, exams, and my future. The worldly things that were so important to me in my twenties are the things that kept me from the kind of relationship with God I so needed at that time in my life.

Roaring Twenties

I opted for the four-and-a-*half*-year plan to complete college. After high school graduation, I landed a retail job and worked the summer before going away to school to contribute to my first year of housing and tuition. I worked part-time on campus all four years; all but the very first semester and full-time every summer. With my parents being divorced, my mom worked a lot of overtime to help out with the added bills along the way (books, tuition, room and board, bus tickets home). She managed to get some grants, but most was racking up on school loans so I worked. I was one of the few students among my circle of friends putting in hours after a day of classes. I studied and wanted to work hard at school. I saw my mom struggle to make ends meet, and I wanted to be sure I could obtain a better-paying job so I never had to depend on a man. Literally, that was my goal.

I started out in the computer lab and then landed a job at the school newspaper in advertising sales by my junior year. *Best move ever.* I *loved* it, and the folks I worked with were my closest friends. I think minimum wage was three dollars per hour when I started at the computer lab. I was elated when it went up to four dollars. *Whoo-hoo!* I made more money at the newspaper on commission, had great friends, and felt like I'd found a place where I belonged. I spent my summers working at the high school where my mom was employed. I was the *skilled* attendant answering the switchboard, delivering mail, and doing data entry for summer school applicants. My mom worked with a fabulous crew, so it was actually fun and we had a lot of laughs.

Throughout my freshman and sophomore year of college, I was still dating my high school boyfriend. We started dating the summer before my senior year. He was a year older and had enrolled in a small Christian college near our hometown. I looked into it, but I had strong reservations about following a boyfriend to college and it was only twenty minutes from home. They even offered me scholarship money to play tennis for them, but the cost of a private college versus public was a defining factor in the decision. By my junior year of college, I broke the relationship off; I'd met someone else and struggled with the long-distance factor. *Does three hours really count as "long distance"?*

The college boyfriend turned into a seven-year relationship. Truth be told, the relationship probably lasted two years too long. He was two years younger than me, so he was still at school after I'd graduated and got a job three hours away. When he finally graduated, we moved in together, but that was short-lived. He cheated, which probably wasn't the first time. He lied, a lot, and I was miserable with him the last couple years. I was so desperate to make it work. I even agreed to us living together because I thought it would be the path to eventually getting married. *Why would you want to marry someone you're miserable with?*

I had literally settled because I thought I was too old to start over and find someone to spend the rest of my life with. *Are you kidding me?* I was twenty-seven. I felt I'd wasted my twenties with the wrong guy, *wanting* him to be the "one" as I watched friends get married. For so long, I thought history dictated destiny, and since I'd been with him seven years, I thought, *that's it. Wrong!* I eventually thanked God for that trial because wanting to plan a wedding is *not* a reason to stay with a guy, especially when your gut tells you this is *not* your future.

I've kept a journal for many years. When I reread the last two years of that relationship, I thought, "Oh my gosh, Laura, snap out of it. You are miserable!" Once out of that relationship, I started to look at the world through a different lens—*mine.* I started listening to music I wanted to listen to, not his. I started to do things I wanted to do, and it was sort of liberating. I was concerned I was in my late twenties, so of course, I wanted very much to meet someone. I thought, "Why did I go so long with so much doubt, ignoring my intuition?" When your gut tells you something isn't right, listen up. That's God speaking to you!

I truly enjoyed college, but similar to settling for the wrong guy and needing a wake-up call, I was complacent with how I spent my weekends at school. In college, we'd have drinks on Friday and Saturday night, listen to music at a party, then go eat burritos at two in the morning. I didn't drink my freshman year of college, but by my sophomore year, I started going out. Any time I drank in excess, I felt guilty about it, knowing I was not pleasing God. I had a memorable conversation with a Catholic friend at school after telling her I'd gone to confession for drinking too much. She said, "But if you do it again and again, every weekend, should you be forgiven?" Good point. My one regret is not going to church on a regular basis through college. I think it would have kept me from drinking too much on the weekends. I was thankful to have a job at the computer lab that kept me from going to parties on Thursday nights when I had to work or on Friday nights when I had to open the lab Saturday morning. Yes, back in the day, we didn't all have personal computers, so students collected in a room to use the school's computers to work on a paper! And get this: we were still using the Dewey decimal system at the library to find books and references to write papers! Microfiche was a form of research. It's crazy to think about what technology has done since 1990.

Ultimately, the drinking was about wanting to belong. I drank to fit in with the crowd. They were having fun, I wanted to have fun. When I look back, drinking consisted of a lot of empty calories combined with a headache or nausea the next day. Did it foster fellowship with strangers I might not have otherwise met and become friends with? *Sure.* A few times, I said "never again" but then followed it up with "the hair of the dog." I guess this is what they mean by "figuring yourself out" in your twenties. You do stupid things over and over and then you grow up. Well, most of us do.

By my junior year, drinking on the weekends was a regular thing. Our tightknit group hung out *all* the time and we did have some fun times, but I still had plenty of fuzzy mornings with a monster head-ache. When I graduated from college, drinking got more responsible primarily because I had to drive myself home. There was one time I know I should not have driven. The next morning, I thanked God for His protection, asked for forgiveness, and vowed to be a better person. When I wasn't the one driving, I had a free pass. I knew I wasn't making God happy by drinking to excess because when you're drinking, you can turn into a potty mouth and tend to gossip or make poor decisions, or you just slur your words and struggle to hold your glass and end up looking like an idiot. I was the "idiot" in this scenario after my seven-year relationship had ended. *Bad coping skills, Laura.* Drinking does not *help* when you are sad; alcohol is a depressant! I blame my Irish heritage for my affinity for beer.

When I started to look at life differently, after surfacing from the gone-on-too-long relationship from college, I wrote down my prayers in my journal. I've kept a journal for years, and writing has always been therapeutic for me. These were prayers about finding the person God wanted me to spend the rest of my life with—His plan, not mine. I went to mass more regularly. I bought a townhouse and established myself as an independent woman, and it felt good to be doing the right things for myself and for God. I felt I had reopened my heart to God and His blessings. Answered prayers come on His time, not ours. When you let go and let God take on your cares, trusting in Him is what opens us up to His presence.

Trusting in God is a moment-by-moment choice. We might trust Him when things are going well and then choose between trust and rebellion against God when things go wrong. It's taken me years to understand I must trust God in *all* circumstances. It's easy to give thanks and trust in Him when things are going right. Real faith kicks in when you can do that when things are not right. I relied on my prayers to send me the companion I so needed. Then Wyatt walked into my life. The happiness barometer was about to skyrocket.

Right Down the Line

In February 2001, I was out at a bar with some friends and my sister. A friend I went to high school and college with bartended, so he'd asked us to stop in now and again. I saw Wyatt up at the bar. I stood next to him to order a drink. I froze, afraid to say anything to strike up a conversation with him. A girl came up to me, and she looked at me, nodded her head his way, and said, "Well, he's cute."

I probably gave her a look like, "Why do you think I'm standing here?" She tapped him on the shoulder, and instantly, I thought, "Well, there goes my chance." Instead, she looked at me, pointed at him, and said, "You two should go dance." So we did.

He tagged along when we went to the next place, and we talked quite a bit. We had a connection, and I knew I wanted to see him again. We had our first kiss that night, and he called a few days later. We had our first date about two weeks after we'd initially met.

We talked on the phone a few times prior to our date, getting to know each other. He was from a very small farming town in Central Illinois. His parents were still married, and he had three siblings. When I first met his family (as his girlfriend), I gravitated to them. I immediately felt a connection to their faith and have given thanks to God time and time again for making me a part of their family.

Our first date was romantic—dinner and then live music at a piano bar. We talked into the wee hours of the night. On our second date, we went to dinner and rented a movie (from Blockbuster!). C'mon, it was 2001. I knew then I was going to fall in love with him. We dated for about six months before we decided to be *exclusive* although I'd decided long before that six-month mark that I had no interest in dating anyone else. We enjoyed going to movies, concerts, Six Flags, car shows, and dinner. It was such a great time in my life.

In 2003, Wyatt had an opportunity to interview for two plant manager positions: one in LA, and the other was Atlanta. The thought of him moving was a little scary. I'd recently changed jobs, so I knew *if* I were to move too, it wouldn't be immediate. He accepted the position and moved to Atlanta in September 2003. He lived in Atlanta right after college, so he was excited about returning to the South. He began looking for a house and bought a beautiful home in December 2003. Once we knew Atlanta was his destination, I started looking for a job. The job I'd started just six months prior to his promotion was not what I'd envisioned. A few months later, my previous employer got wind of our situation and asked me to come back, as if I'd never left the company, *and* work from wherever I wanted! What a blessing! I gave my notice and moved to Atlanta in March 2004. Six months apart was tough, but the longest we went without seeing each other was only two weeks. I'd fly down to Atlanta, or he'd come back up to Chicago. The first time I had to go home on a Sunday evening after a weekend in Atlanta, I was just sick to my stomach. I hated being apart from him.

When I moved to Atlanta, Wyatt moved out of the house he'd just bought. Easier for him to find a temporary place to stay with a friend than me! I didn't know anyone in Atlanta. He was so thoughtful in his house hunting to ask me what kinds of features I wanted in a house. We'd had conversations about marriage, so my decision to sell my townhouse and pick up and move to Atlanta for him was with the understanding that marriage was in our future. I was just anxiously waiting for him to pop the question.

Wyatt's often told the story about how I'd be depressed every Sunday after a weekend had gone by and he hadn't asked. He had secretly been doing all this research to find the right diamond and setting. When he had decided he would ask me, he had a bit of poison ivy from working out in the yard, which put a wrench in his plan. He gets poison ivy *annually*! He didn't want to ask as he had a spot on his face (poor guy) and postponed a few more days to the weekend when his sisters were coming down to visit.

He completely caught me off guard; I never imagined he'd ask me with his two younger sisters in town. We'd gone to a race at Road Atlanta. Wyatt is a car guy, so those who know him were not surprised at the location. When I say he's a car guy, I mean he has been living and breathing cars since childhood. Here I'd been envisioning he'd pop the question over dinner or somewhere romantic, but instead, we had the roaring sounds of race cars flying by as we walked out to a grassy spot on one of the turns of the track. He got down on one knee. His sister was in on it and filmed the whole thing. We had driven two cars to the race, so one sister was in the car with him. On the way, she asked about our relationship, "You think Laura is the one?"

He said, "Funny you should ask. I have a diamond ring burning a hole in my pocket right now. I'm going to ask Laura to marry me *today*!"

She had to keep it a secret for a few hours, bursting at the seams with excitement. At one point, Wyatt's other sister sensed something, asking her sister, "Are you okay? You're acting weird."

It made it ten times more special to have them there with us to celebrate May 15, 2004. We plan things out in our heads, and sometimes when it doesn't go as planned, it turns out even better. In his mind, a man plans his course, but the Lord directs his steps (Prov. 16:9, NAB).

We'd always talked about getting married in the fall up in Illinois, so we utilized my mad skills to get it all done in five months and we got married in October 2004. I was finishing my master's degree *and* planning a wedding so it was a hectic time, but it was full of excitement. I remember thinking my time had finally arrived—a time to be truly happy. It felt like a fresh start leaving a lot of pain in the past. I felt truly blessed.

Wyatt is the love of my life. If I was ever stranded on a deserted island, he is the one person I would want with me, not just because I love him so much but because he knows so much! I used to say if I was on a deserted island, I'd need a pen and a piece of paper to make a list of to-dos. The project manager in me would be able to identify, prioritize, and delegate tasks. Great, but that doesn't help us *survive!*

Wyatt can build or fix anything. He would be able to build us a hut, make us a raft, and create rope from bamboo trees like Tom Hanks in *Castaway*. He'd know how to make a funnel contraption to catch rainwater, and he'd have a strategy for hunting animals or would fashion a fishing pole from a stick. He is so smart, so handy, and so good-looking and is a hardworking, faith-filled man. He was raised Catholic, and we went to mass while we were dating, which I just loved. That kind of relationship, where God was a part of it, was everything I'd ever wanted. God truly had a hand in bringing us together. I remember my mom saying she was so thankful Wyatt and I had talked about so many different scenarios before getting married. We discussed how we would raise and discipline our kids, manage finances, where we'd travel to, and how we would split chores and household responsibilities. Not discussing these types of things can be a surprise for couples down the road. We went into marriage with a strong foundation in our faith and equal expectations. God blessed our marriage in His house and our love for each other and, for God, grew every day.

When Tristan had his accident, we were all at home. Wyatt was the one who took on the most difficult part—to try to revive him. I will forever be thankful to Wyatt for his ability to do what he did and for his quick thinking and perseverance in our worst nightmare. I dialed 911 and somehow got them to our house. Colton prayed. I didn't cry. I couldn't cry. Not even as I sat in the front seat of the ambulance. And I remember thinking, "What is going on? I'm not crying?" My adrenaline was through the roof, yet I called my mom and asked her to call the entire family and *pray.* People later told me, that's shock. In my state of shock, on my deserted island, Wyatt was right there with me, taking action. *It's been you, Wyatt, right down the line.*

We spent our honeymoon in Italy. It was my first time overseas. Getting married *and* getting to travel to Europe just felt like the biggest gift God could have given me at that time. We had an amazing time visiting the Amalfi coast, staying in Positano, and scouring Rome. We visited churches, monuments, museums, the Vatican, the island of Capri—it was a dream come true for me. After our honeymoon, we decided we would try to take big trips to get back to Europe every few years. We haven't been back to the Amalfi coast but have been overseas three more times. Carving out the time and taking these trips as a couple put our focus on each other, which we felt was crucial to our parenting abilities. Being a strong, loving, united front kept us on the same page for how we managed work, kids, all other responsibilities, and obstacles that came our way.

After three big trips in twelve years, we agreed we would stay stateside for future vacations. We had started talking about all the next trips we'd like to take to Washington, DC, the Grand Canyon, Montana, Maine, you name it. There are plenty of places we still haven't been. We took the boys on lots of other weekend getaways, camping trips, or spring break vacations to Florida, Illinois, Missouri, and Tennessee. Travel has always been a treat for me; I love it. Growing up, I went on *one* family vacation and one other trip to Michigan with my mom, sister, and friends. When I got into project management with my company, I loved when I had an opportunity to travel for a client meeting. I'm over that now (business travel is not all it's cracked up to be!), but in my single days, I enjoyed it. I was motivated to work hard to afford vacations I never got to take as a kid.

Traveling back up to Illinois to see family was an easy flight from Atlanta—one hour and fifty minutes to be exact. We started racking up points and put all our expenses on an airline credit card to further the freebies. The kids were no strangers to an airport.

Our favorite airport story is when our son Colton was just a baby, and the four of us flew up to Milwaukee for a weekend. Colton was awful, cried the whole flight, and fought the need to fall asleep. I think I literally asked someone if there was a priest on the plane; this child seemed possessed, grunting and flailing his body. Parents, you know this move, where they arch their back. This move is often used when attempting to refuse a secure belting-in when trying to get them into the car seat. We got off the "worst flight of our lives" and began walking briskly, keeping up with the flow heading to baggage claim. Tristan was about three and a half years old and lost his grip and dropped his rolly suitcase he was pulling behind him. A man in the oncoming traffic tripped over it, sending the poor soul up over the case and onto the floor.

I think we all saw it play out in slow motion with that long "noooooooooo" kind of reaction. Wyatt immediately went to the aid of this man and lent a hand for him to stand back up. In that instant, we all realized the man he'd tripped had a prosthetic leg. Tristan yelled out, "Hey... that's not a real leg!" like he'd made a great discovery and this guy was not about to pull one over on us!

I look at Wyatt, eyes wide open like, "He did *not* just say that." Apologizing, I swung the stroller around and headed for the bathroom with Colton at warp speed—"Abort mission! Abort mission!" As I left Wyatt in my dust, he grabbed Tristan and the infamous Hot Wheels suitcase and left the scene before Tristan had a chance to say something else, perhaps a jab about the man's haircut or how he was dressed that would really add to our embarrassment! Make it stop!

A few college-age girls who sat behind us on the plane, now watching our debacle unfold, just laughed at the whole situation as our bad luck doubled before we could even get to baggage claim. I believe we gave Tristan a serious talk about being more polite. "Honey, it's not nice to tell everyone about this man's circumstances." This type of conversation falls into the same bucket as when Colton asked the *female* nurse at his pediatrician's office why she had a mustache. Out of the mouths of babes. I ignored that one as if it never graced our ears. Another one of those "get me out of here as soon as possible" moments.

We've all had moments like that. God has a sense of humor, huh? The embarrassment wears off, and now they are funny stories we cherish. Wyatt has watched me for years fill my journals with all kinds of stories that were our life with those two boys, and when bad things happened, I used to say "God has a plan." We struggle with God's plan now. How could *this* be His plan? It's not laid out in a project plan for me to see what comes next, but we try hard every day to walk by faith, not by sight (2 Cor. 5:7, NAB).

Our walk by faith has included a few obstacles like that suitcase on the ground but nothing we didn't pop back up from. I can't get on a plane and jet-set my way out of this situation though. Believe me, we tried. You could drive or fly to the ends of the earth, and your pain travels with you. You can't leave this kind of pain at home. There is no vacation, no promotion at work, no amount of money that can take this pain away. People say "time," but time doesn't do anything except allow you to accept your new normal is an emotional prison sentence. Wyatt and I held onto each other and relied on our faith and the strength of our marriage to carry us through this season, waiting for Jesus to show up and stretch out His hand and help us up from the floor. We both wanted nothing but a first-class ticket out of here and into heaven.

Becoming Parents

They say you are never fully prepared to be a parent. That's because it is the toughest job on the planet, but *the* most rewarding one ever. Wyatt and I had decided we would try for a family as soon as we were married. Six months after we tied the knot, I was pregnant! I remember walking around, and in my head, I kept repeating, "I'm pregnant. Oh my gosh, I'm pregnant." I wanted to tell *everyone* but waited until we were six weeks along before telling family and then closer to the end of the first trimester before we officially shared the news. I had morning sickness for ten straight weeks, and it wasn't just in the morning. I'd call it "all-day sickness." It was a routine pregnancy until I was about thirty-seven weeks, and we found out Tristan was in a breech position. This news came after doing a breathing class (a class to learn how to breathe, really?) and anticipating a standard birth. I'm a planner, so I can get caught up with what I've planned for and try not to stress about a blip in the plan. I fail.

We went to the hospital on New Year's Day 2006 for a procedure to try to turn the baby. Construction on the hospital had caused the wing we were in to lose access to oxygen, so we had to reschedule for the *next* day. We went in January 2, 2006, and my ob-gyn and a fetal specialist tried turning Tristan, unsuccessfully—a frightening and somewhat painful experience. They got him transverse, which means his body was across my belly. They let go, and he literally floated right back to the position he was in when they started (head stuck pressing into my ribs on my right side, feet down). Well, that didn't work.

We scheduled the C-section for a week out, but my water broke a day later on the afternoon of January 3, 2006. I'd already had my bags packed as they told me to "be ready" when we did the inversion. Wyatt was about forty minutes away at work. I'd just taken a shower and gone to the bathroom. I was standing in my underwear and a top in my master closet when "swoosh." I thought, "Did I just pee? No, I couldn't have. I *just* peed. My water broke!" I called my ob-gyn to tell her, and she advised I come *right* in so we "didn't have a foot hanging out." Quite the visual. I called my neighbor who had just delivered her son six weeks earlier. Her husband was gone, so she offered to drive me. She packed up her little guy, and we were off. I called my mom on the way.

She said, "What are you doing?"

I said, "My mascara. I can't go in looking like this."

Right, 'cause after they cut my stomach open, it will be a good thing that I stopped to put mascara on! Pfffft. Wyatt and my close friend met me at the hospital where they quickly got me into pre-op. They gave me an epidural, and within just hours of my water breaking, Tristan Paul Schupbach arrived at 6:28 p.m. Since he was breech, there were a few seconds where the doctor had trouble getting him out. The mood in the operating room went from normal delivery to panic for a few seconds. She kicked the rolling chair back and yelled out instructions. She said I had a heart-shaped uterus, and my tailbone cupped up, making it obvious why he couldn't turn and get into a head-down position after he reached a certain size. Who knew! Tristan had to go to the NICU for a bit, and I had the shakes (and itching) from the epidural wearing off, but I just stared at his picture—a Polaroid they'd taken after cleaning him up. They brought him over to me before wheeling me into recovery, so I gave him a kiss but didn't have the chance to hold him.

Once they got me into my hospital room four hours later, I told Wyatt, "Do not come back until you have my baby." Our very first nurse introduced herself, and her name was "Blessing." God's presence seemed to fill the room. I tried nursing him for the first time, and I thought, "This is it. I am a mom, and God has blessed me with a perfectly healthy baby boy." Next to getting married to the love of my life, it was *the* happiest moment.

We brought Tristan home a few days later. We kept the Pack 'n Play in the living room for easy diaper changes. The first night home, we were changing his diaper and heard something.

"What is that noise? Oh my gosh, he's *peeing*! He's peeing on the wall!"

A stream was going up over his head, hitting the wall. Wyatt went to put a gauze pad down to stop the stream, and Tristan let out a wail. After a circumcision, poor little guy was probably still tender there. Wyatt started crying; I was crying. We were like bumbling idiots thinking, "How did the hospital let us take this child home? Where is the instruction manual!"

We found our way, and I loved maternity leave. I absolutely loved that 100 percent of my day was dedicated to caring for this small, dependent person. I never knew how much God loved us until I became a mother, and I finally got it. By eleven weeks, Tristan was sleeping through the night, and I'd started weaning him off of breast milk.

I have such precious memories of nursing my boys in the middle of the night. At the time, I was exhausted, but everything was quiet and I'd sit rocking back and forth with only the light from a nightlight. It was so peaceful.

For what it's worth, breastfeeding then was not what it is today. I would have probably done it longer if I'd had privacy at work to pump. It was painful to start nursing, but within the first couple weeks, I could see how easily it could be to continue. In 2006, it was not the norm to stay in the room where company was visiting and just start nursing. We didn't have those cute wraps to cover up. I had to excuse myself every time, so that contributed to reasons for weaning him onto formula when I went back to work after twelve weeks off. Now I see women nursing as they are walking through the grocery store or standing in line at the amusement park. Huh? *How do you do that?*

Tristan was an amazing toddler. He was spot-on with his development. He took his first steps days before his first birthday. We'd weaned him off the bottle onto sippy cups right at one year. He was potty-trained by two, talking, singing, and capturing the attention of all his family, our friends, and caretakers at our daycare. It was about this age, I started "Hugs, kisses, high fives"—our signature goodbye when I'd drop him off and the last thing we'd say to each other after bedtime prayers. As he got older, I'd include it on written notes as "OX^5" whether I stuck it in his lunchbox or left a note on the fridge. "Hugs, Kisses, High Fives" is on Tristan's headstone at his grave site.

His brother, Colton, arrived November 13, 2008. Similar to my first pregnancy, I had ten weeks of morning sickness. This pregnancy wasn't breech, but my ob-gyn had advised a C-section based on the complications I'd had earlier. My water broke two weeks before my scheduled C-section; this time, it was four in the morning! I'd just come downstairs to read a book after being awake for quite some time. I got onto the couch, curled up with a blanket and a book, and "swoosh." My water broke. We called my friend to come watch Tristan and get him to daycare while we went to the hospital. I hadn't had labor pains with Tristan, but with Colton, they started immediately.

I called my mom and could *barely* get through a conversation without grunting for twenty seconds every few minutes. This is NOTHING compared to the *hours* of labor I've heard other friends went through, so I was not complaining. My experience with this epidural was *not* like the first. First time around, I felt a little pinch and then a cold sensation drop down into either side of my hips. I thought, that was easy! This time around, I could feel *everything*, and they kept asking me to tell them whether I felt it on the left or the right. I was yelling "left," sobbing *"right," "left,"* then cried out, "Wyatt, this isn't like the first one." I was a mess and then it was done. I collected myself and said, "Sorry for, um, kind of losing it there." I figured I had a *seasoned* anesthesiologist in 2006, and this time, it must have been a first-year? Or perhaps they were just having an off day.

I went in thinking I was having a girl, so I was delightfully surprised when Wyatt told me, "It's another boy." Colton came out with

Wyatt's cleft chin—so handsome, so loved. The next day, he met his big brother, Tristan, for the first time.

Tristan always talked about how he remembered the hospital gown I was wearing and that I cried when he held his brother for the first time. Tristan was an amazing big brother. He cared for and taught Colton so much. One of our favorite memories of Tristan is the one time I walked in on him with Colton on the changing table, diaper off. I said, "Tristan, *what* are you doing?"

He said "Mom, I've seen you do it a thousand times." So confident at such a young age.

Life with those two boys, man... If you could bottle it up and sell the emotion, I'd be a millionaire. Being the only ones down in Atlanta, we traveled up north to see family often, so the boys were no strangers to an airport or airplanes. The boys had special relationships with their grandparents, aunts, uncles, and cousins despite living far away. They came to visit a couple times a year, and we went up north about three times a year. We vacationed together at times too. In between trips, we worked; we lived, and enjoyed our life in Atlanta. My job was stressful but, I had decided pre-kids I couldn't be a stay-at-home mom. I'd be bored, and I felt it was best for the boys that I continue to maintain my career. I needed to be busy; structured. I felt I made a healthy decision to go to work while they went to daycare. I used to say I was a better mom *because* I worked.

Our daycare had a huge park, structured playtime, meal times, nap time, Bible story time, swimming lessons in the summer, and even Spanish classes. They became our extended family. The front desk knew the names of every kid and parent there. Added benefit was if you were in daycare, you had a guaranteed spot in their pre-K program. Parents would line up the night *before* outside the daycare to secure a place in their pre-K program. The first time I saw this, I thought there was a parade or something that morning. Here were these parents with lawn chairs and blankets and coolers for snacks. Nope, no parade; they were just willing to pull an all-nighter to get in! They'd been a Christian-based, family-owned business for over twenty-five years when we started Tristan there. I'd waited a year to get Tristan into daycare there.

I worked my way up the corporate ladder but struggled with mom-guilt on top of pressure from a high-stress job. Two times, I'd reached a breaking point and was *this close* to handing in my resignation. The pressure, high expectations, long hours—I couldn't handle it. Each time I was so close to throwing in the towel, I'd get a raise or a promotion, and I'd stick it out a little longer. When I think about the worldly things that kept me working, it was title, money, and recognition (aka pride). All things I'd give up in a heartbeat if I could have my son back. "Humble yourselves before the Lord, and He will exalt you" (James 4:10, NAB).

Come 2012, I was in a position I'd strived for most of my career; I finally felt I'd achieved my goals. The fast pace continued at work, but come 2016, I'd set healthy boundaries for myself and was picking up the boys from after-school-care about 5:15 p.m. every day. Our weeknights had become busier with both boys in sports. I'd pick them up, and we'd have minutes to wolf down a snack, get changed, and get to the swimming pool, football field, or the basketball court. After fall and winter, we always took the spring season off. Getting onto a field or court by 5:30 or 6 p.m. was challenging. I was so thankful to work from home, which I started full-time after Colton was born. How did other parents who worked full-time with an hour-long commute manage sports? Wyatt's travel had increased tremendously, and I was a single mom two weeks out of every month for 2015 to 2016.

I complained about the schedule, yet I would give up my arms and legs, everything I have, to get back to that time in our life. *Take us back, Lord.* I've prayed it so many times, for God to bend time and take us back. I loved watching the boys play sports, whether it was in our backyard or an organized team. The happiness meter just kept going up as my boys grew. My marriage and my job as a mom were top priority in my life. Several times, I'd catch myself working while they were at practice, and I'd say, "Stop. Put down the phone. These moments are precious."

The Accident

I made a point to give you the background on me so you'll have an understanding of who I was, where my faith journey had taken me, and what trials I'd had in my life leading up to my *perfect* life with Wyatt and the boys. It was just that—perfect. When I found Wyatt, I felt my suffering was behind me. We had fifteen straight years of bliss—now a defined season of my life as another season rolled in. This one, not so perfect.

January 15, 2017 started out as a regular Sunday for us. We got up early to go to 7:30 a.m. mass. Tristan was serving as an altar boy. He'd only been doing it since November, but I just loved seeing him participating in the mass like that. He had told me it was really cool to be on the altar during mass and said, "Mom, did you know he washes his hands before communion?" My, how one's perspective changes when you get up close. I'd gone to communion that morning, returned to my pew, and prayed prayers of thanksgiving as I always had. One prayer in particular I prayed that morning was thanks to God for not giving us the kind of trial I'd seen others suffer. I had prayed this prayer before but not often, so it stands out. I prayed it *that* morning, and then our worst nightmare came true. How is that even possible?

We had thirty minutes in between mass and religion class, so we ran to the store and then back over to church to drop the boys off. I'd come back at 10:15 a.m. to pick them up. I had my arm around Tristan as we were walking down the hall toward the door to the parking lot and told him I think he literally grew an inch since Christmas. He seemed so tall to me, my little man.

Every Sunday after mass, I'd pick up the newspaper and head in for bacon and eggs. Wyatt didn't cook during the week. If I needed him to, he'd "heat" something, but Sunday mornings were his thing. Bacon, eggs, toast, everybody gets fried eggs, don't go asking for scrambled now. You get what you get, and you don't throw a fit. At least that's a motto I liked to keep around the house. Years ago, I'd instituted "No TV Sundays." For years, our routine was to come home from mass, have breakfast, read the paper, and then go about whatever errands or play in the backyard sans television. I had grown to cherish Sunday mornings. Come Sunday night, we did watch a movie. Sunday night has always been movie night since Wyatt and I were dating, and we always picked a feel-good movie to help us prep for another week ahead.

After breakfast that Sunday, Tristan ran upstairs to grab all the money he'd saved from Christmas, past birthdays, and mowing the lawn. He wanted to combine it with gift cards he received the night before when we celebrated his eleventh birthday with his close friends. Tristan turned eleven on January 3, 2017, but we'd only been home two days since coming back from a trip up north for Christmas and an extended trip to Wisconsin snowmobiling for New Years. We pushed his birthday celebration with his friends out to January 14. We took ten of his friends to a rock climbing facility after having pizza at the house and cupcakes after arriving home.

On the way to the rock climbing place, the sun was just going down. I had seven eleven-year-old boys in my car, so you can imagine the noise level. At one point, Tristan said, "Guys, guys, quiet down, Look at that sunset!"

I looked at him, a little bewildered that he would stop and notice God's creation with the distraction of all his buds in the car laughing and singing and joking around. Tristan put his hand on my knee from where he sat in the passenger seat and just gave me that smile. The moment is frozen in my mind. That was Tristan. He could rise above all the noise of this world and bring you to an awareness of the present moment.

One by one, parents came to pick up the boys after we'd arrived home. It was the first time we'd done a party like that where we took the boys somewhere without asking parents to drop off and pick up *at* the location. Tristan wanted to have more time with his friends; he enjoyed playing with them before and after rock climbing.

Back to that Sunday morning. I ran to Target to get a few things and checked out at 12:41 p.m. Tristan had left me a voicemail at 12:20 p.m., asking if he could go shopping with our neighbor and his mom to spend some of his birthday money around 3:30 p.m. when he would be home from a friend's birthday party. I'd forgotten about this voicemail for three months until I listened to it again, not realizing it would be Tristan's voice behind the "Wyatt voicemail" from January 15, 2017. "Hey, Mom. It's me, Tristan... You don't have to, but I think it would be cool if you came shopping too! Bye. Love you." I cherish the videos and this voicemail with his precious voice.

Tristan counted his money and gift cards and had decided he wanted to get a hover board. He got out his iPad mini we'd bought him for school that year and started searching online. Since he was going to buy the hover board online, we diverted the shopping trip. If only... *Would he still be here if I'd let him go? Are our days numbered when we're born?* I was back home by 1:00 p.m., in time to take Tristan to his friend's birthday party. It was a beautiful day, which was wonderful for January, especially since we'd had snow in Atlanta the week prior! Tristan and Colton were out sledding with the neighbors on January 7, and now Tristan was off to play football in shorts? Gotta love the South.

I dropped Tristan off at 1:30 p.m. and came home to join Wyatt and Colton for a Cub Scouts meeting. We drove separate so Wyatt and Colton could stay at the meeting, and I left in time to get Tristan by 3:30 p.m. Our friends hosted the party for their son whom Tristan had known since he was two. When I picked Tristan up, the mom was doting on Tristan as she always did—one of the sweetest moms I know. As Tristan and I walked back to my car, I put my arm around him, and he said, "Mom, I had more fun than I thought I would."

I said, "What do you mean, bud?"

He said, "Well, I didn't know many kids, but that didn't matter."

I said, "Oh, I wouldn't think so, Tristan. You've never had a problem blending in no matter the crowd."

As we drove home, he'd asked about how I'd learned to drive a stick shift. Just a random conversation tapping into the mind of an eleven-year-old. I told him how Papa (my dad) insisted I learn how to drive a stick before an automatic so I could drive an eighteen-wheeler in an emergency if I needed to. Never have had to drive a truck yet, but it's still been a good skill to have. Thanks, Dad. I loved teaching the boys anything I could to make them self-sufficient even if knowledge of driving a stick shift wouldn't apply to Tristan for five more years. We talked about the balance between the clutch and the gas and using neutral to slow down while pressing the brake without having to use the clutch. He was like a sponge and retained information so well. He was an A student. I most enjoyed how he could memorize his lines for the play and easily regurgitate lyrics and movie quotes. He was witty and had begun to drop one-liner movie quotes in the context of every-day conversation.

We got home about 3:45 p.m., and I was surprised to see Wyatt and Colton were already home from the Cub Scout meeting. The next two hours are a little fuzzy. Wyatt was working on the downstairs guest bathroom, chipping up the old tile floor, so it was *loud*. Dust was everywhere. The boys were playing outside and had been in and out of the house. I can sit in the living room, and since our house has a lot of windows, I can see out the front *and* out the back. The boys knew the boundaries established years ago about not going into the street. We are only the second house into the neighborhood and folks drive too fast, so playing in the front yard always had its rules.

At one point in the bathroom project that day, Wyatt and Tristan carried the old vanity over to the neighbor's house across the street. Our neighbor was remodeling his garage and had a dumpster on his driveway and offered we use it for scrap from our bathroom. Tristan was Wyatt's helper all the time—so strong, a like-minded engineer in the making. He was a clone, a mini-me, of Wyatt, and I loved how they would interact like a team. Wyatt taught Tristan things I didn't even know how to do. Tristan was his apprentice. What a hard worker he had become, doing work 99 percent of other kids his age would not even attempt.

I was reading a magazine on the couch, needing to get up soon to start dinner. All of a sudden, I heard Wyatt shouting, "No, no, no, no, no, no, no!" It wasn't a mad voice; it was a frightened, panicked voice. I opened the front door, and Colton was standing ten feet in front of me on the front lawn, facing the side of the house, crying.

I yelled, "What's wrong? What happened?" My first thoughts were, "Someone got hit by a car." As I ran off the porch into the front, I turned to the right to see Tristan in Wyatt's arms, unconscious. I thought, "Oh my gosh, he knocked himself out. He hit the tree, riding the little zip line Wyatt had put up years before." I ran inside to get my phone. Seconds later, I ran out, and Wyatt had put Tristan in the back of his car, then quickly took him out and laid him on the ground next to our driveway. He immediately started CPR. I called 911 and fumbled entering the numbers before my stupid four-digit code to unlock my phone. I got on the phone at 5:44 p.m., frantically gave our address, and begged for help. I wasn't crying. My heart was beating a million miles a second.

As I type this, my heart is racing just recounting the details even though they've run through my head a thousand times. Colton was still crying. I can't remember what I said to him. Our neighbor came running across the street. Our other neighbor ran over confused about what was going on. Matt was by Wyatt's side as he continued CPR. The 911 operator had me count 1-2-3-4 and asked if there was a pulse. I yelled out, "Is there a pulse?"

Matt turned around, eyes down, and just whispered, "No."

I remember seeing spit come out of Tristan's mouth and thought he might be coming to, but it was merely the pressure of Wyatt doing CPR. These memories are stained in my mind forever. All the while, Colton sat in front of the house and prayed. My little prayer warrior sprang into action immediately. I am so proud of him. I can hear the sirens. They're coming. They're almost here. "Run out to the road, and flag them down," she said. "Stay on the phone with me until they're there."

Once they were at Wyatt's side, they took over. Wyatt's hands just ran through his hair, dumfounded at what was happening, and eyes wide open in total shock as he literally walked in small circles on the driveway. Seven minutes. He did CPR for seven minutes, and it felt like an eternity.

When they arrived, they asked what happened while the others started treating Tristan. Wyatt said, "Asphyxiation."

I looked at him and said, "What?" I had no idea. That's when I realized what was going on. The rope from the zip line had gotten around his neck. They got a pulse and started to put Tristan onto the stretcher to take him in the ambulance. I snapped into a more conscious state and said, "I'm going with my son!" I ran inside, grabbed my shoes, and had them in my hand when I climbed into the front seat of the ambulance with nothing but my phone. I couldn't see or hear anything from the front of the ambulance. The woman driver called in our ETA and advised which hospital we were headed to. I called my Mom and asked her to call the entire family to pray. I told her it was serious—*pray!* I still wasn't crying.

I was ushered into a room at the hospital while the trauma team got to work. I got down on my knees in that private room and prayed by myself. Wyatt and Colton arrived minutes later compliments of a ride from our neighbor, another faith-filed man who didn't leave Wyatt's side through the whole thing. I was on and off the phone with my mom and then my sister-in-law. We had the hospital call our pastor, and a pastor from a neighboring parish arrived. As I walked with him to see Tristan in the trauma room, I felt the prayers and stares of everyone behind the desk. He gave Tristan last rites. This was not happening. I begged the trauma team to please save him. I was able to talk to Tristan, but he was unresponsive. They Life-Flighted Tristan to the Children's Hospital of Atlanta.

The sound of a helicopter will never be heard the same. I'm instantly brought back to that moment *every* time. We stood outside the ER doors and waited until they took off. The whole operation of preparing to move him was elaborate, and I am forever grateful to the team of doctors, nurses, and pilots who helped us that evening. Our neighbor drove us to Children's Hospital. I sat in the back seat with Colton praying, and I have no idea what Matt and Wyatt discussed in the front seat. I got the call from the helicopter team that they'd arrived, and when we got there, they ushered us into another private room and had someone take Colton. The first doctor we saw said to prepare ourselves for severe neurological damage *if* he survived. Again, we just grunted in disbelief. *No!* Not Tristan, *not* Tristan. I kicked the couch in the room we were in. I screamed, "*No*, this is *not* happening, not to Tristan."

They let us come to the trauma room. They had him on support, and Wyatt and I prayed and stood by Tristan's side. I told those in the room that he was an amazing son, brother, athlete, actor, and an altar boy. I begged them to save him. I begged God for a miracle.

Wyatt handled questions from a police officer and the hospital admittance while I sat in a chair outside the trauma room looking in on Tristan. A single metal chair that wasn't normally in the hospital hallway was placed there for me. We were waiting to go up to ICU. Nearly three hours after I'd made the frantic 911 call, we were in an ICU unit. Tristan was on an oscillator that kept his lungs open to provide as much oxygen as possible. It was loud and clanked like a nervous person tapping a keyboard over and over and over. We prayed for a miracle over and over, but we also prayed for God's will and our acceptance of His will at the same time. I repeated over and over in my head, "I surrender to you, Lord. My son is in your hands and always has been." Chaplains prayed with us. Nurses prayed with us. We filled that room with the Holy Spirit and waited. They had to get him transitioned to a regular ventilator before they could move him down to get a CT scan and really know what was going on.

My mom and my sister began to arrange travel to Atlanta. My sister said they could get here Tuesday. I called them and said, "You need to come in Monday. We may lose him." Simultaneously, Wyatt's sister, brother, and parents were arranging travel. They arrived first about nine in the morning, just twelve hours since we'd been brought into the ICU. My sister brought her whole family, my brother-in-law, and her two boys, with my Mom arriving early afternoon. Everyone broke down the second they laid eyes on us. I'll never forget my brother-in-law; he just started sobbing when he saw me. We were starting to see the impact Tristan had on so many of our family and friends.

At one o'clock that first night, we called our neighbor to bring Colton back to the hospital. We were beginning to prepare ourselves for the worst. Monsignor, our pastor, came to the hospital. Our friend drove through the night straight from Florida and never left the hospital. More friends arrived and slept between two chairs pushed together in a bright waiting room. One of my close friends, a bridesmaid from our wedding, traveled from Illinois, then neighbors began coming by, coworkers, parishioners from our church. Whether they were staying, just stopping by, or dropping off food, it was a constant flow of support. My one neighbor arranged for rooms at a nearby hotel. We were all prepared to wait and pray for a miracle, no matter how long it took.

I didn't eat. I couldn't sleep. Wyatt and I shared a bench about two-thirds the size of a twin-sized bed. We didn't fit unless one of us was lying on our side. The pain of what we were going through was unbelievable. If I dozed off, I'd wake up thinking, "Please let it be a nightmare."

The hospital arranged for Colton to do a handprint on one side of a canvas, and they did the same for Tristan. I couldn't believe I was making a decision on one last memento to capture the size and shape of their hands. I can't do this; I can't live without him. As we waited, Wyatt read a book Tristan had received for Christmas called *The Boy Who Knew Everything*. Everyone prayed and talked to Tristan. I'd beg God, even bargain with Him, to save my son. Bring him back just the way he was. Let him wake up and say, "Mom? What happened?"

That moment never came. They put leads on his head to track brain activity, but I never got any definitive information. The neurologist advised that with an incident like this, having been deprived of oxygen, brain damage was very likely. They had to wait. How is this happening? What was he doing? How did this happen? He's perfectly healthy, a straight-A student, a star basketball player with a game this weekend and the lead in the school play for the second year in a row. We had rehearsals to get to and only weeks left to be the best Captain Hook there was. We had basketball practice and a game coming up. Not this; this was not happening.

We became rather friendly with the nurses, especially two in particular. They allowed me to bathe Tristan, my sweet boy, and wash his hair. I told the nurse about his stinky feet and told lots of other stories to the nurses as they were in and out. They are true angels here on earth. Jane, Jen, you two were amazing to us and to Tristan, and we will never forget you and your kindness.

By Tuesday night, our close friends had orchestrated a prayer vigil for Tristan in the park—the same park where he played football and basketball and went on walks and runs and swung on swings. These were friends with an eleven-year-old themselves. We were on the same basketball team, and our boys grew up together. Seeing a picture of hundreds of students and families gathered at the park lighting candles and saying prayers for a miracle was overwhelming.

The following morning, friends from the drama club got together to pray for Tristan, and that night, a prayer service was held at our church. I'd reached out to our local Christian radio station, 104.7 The Fish, and started exchanging texts with one of the DJs—more prayers. At this point, there were thousands praying for Tristan. He'd been added to prayer chains while priests and nuns had been contacted all over the United States, requesting prayers. I just kept repeating, "Thy will be done," mixed in with "Bring him back to us, just as he was." Let him wake up and say, "Mom? What happened? Where am I?" Constant prayer, reading the Bible, even bargaining with God. Was this a punishment for something I'd done? No, God doesn't punish. He meets us in our circumstances, but "why?" Why us? Why Tristan? Please, grant us a miracle, Lord, please.

I played music for Tristan in his hospital room often—all the songs we would listen to in my car or ones I'd play while cooking or having coffee on Saturday mornings in the kitchen. Those songs, they were a large part of my prayer life over the last eleven years. We would belt out songs from The Fish artists like Newsboys, Jamie Grace, MercyMe, Laura Story, and Johnny Diaz. The lyrics were scripture. Tristan and Colton knew all the words.

I could always tell if the boys had been in Wyatt's car based on the songs they were reciting—Van Halen, AC/DC, Weezer, any seventies rock. I could tell if they'd heard songs at school that weren't appropriate because if they weren't from The Fish or Dad's selection, they heard it elsewhere. Nothing warmed my heart more than when the boys knew all the lyrics to our Fish songs. I'd catch them humming those songs and think, "God's Word is with us, always."

One song in particular that helped me focus was "Thy Will Be Done" by Hillary Scott.

> I'm so confused
> I know I heard you loud and clear
> So, I followed through
> Somehow I ended up here
>
> I don't wanna think
> I may never understand
> That my broken heart is a part of your plan
> When I try to pray
>
> All I got is hurt and these four words
> Thy will be done
> Thy will be done
> Thy will be done
>
> I know you're good
> But this don't feel good right now
> And I know you think
> Of things I could never think about

It's hard to count it all joy
Distracted by the noise
Just trying to make sense
Of all your promises
Sometimes I gotta stop
Remember that you're God
And I am not
So...

Thy will be done
Thy will be done
Thy will be done

Like a child on my knees all that comes to me is
Thy will be done
Thy will be done
Thy will

I know you see me
I know you hear me, Lord
Your plans are for me
Goodness you have in store

I know you hear me
I know you see me, Lord
Your plans are for me
Goodness you have in store
So

Thy will be done

Thy will be done
Thy will be done

Like a child on my knees
All that comes to me is
Thy will be done
Thy will be done
Thy will be done

I know you see me
I know you hear me, Lord

They told us the CT scan he got when he was initially admitted wasn't worth anything as the brain would swell, and that's where the real damage happens. They told us a true assessment would present itself in the next forty-eight to seventy-two hours. We had to wait it out. Our nurse made a sign for our ICU sliding door: "PRAY FOR TRISTAN." It had a picture of a Ferrari and the University of Illinois emblem on it. People changed their Facebook profile picture to a "14," his basketball number, with "Pray for Tristan." So many people, storming the gates of heaven on his behalf. I'd told myself time and time again, I will stay here and live in this hospital for as long as it takes. Nothing else mattered. Not the job I'd put first so many times, not the appointments, not the house that always had to be in tip-top shape if someone visited. None of it mattered. I had hope that surpassed all, and I envisioned having conversations with Tristan in the future about the accident and the time we spent in the hospital with him. I had hope we would look back on this and talk about it like other lessons learned in life.

Wednesday night, we were downstairs taking a break and visiting with friends who had brought food. As we got back upstairs to ICU, my sister-in-law rushed us into the room. Something was wrong. About fifteen people were in the room, literally—nurses, a nurse practitioner, a doctor, people I hadn't seen before. I felt so naïve. I knew nothing about the drugs they were using to stabilize Tristan. This team, Tristan's army at Children's Hospital, they were just amazing. Watching them spring into action was reassuring. I placed my trust in God to guide them to do what was best.

They speculated Tristan's brain had swollen causing the reaction his body had (a change in temperature, change in blood pressure, you name it, bells and lights were going off on all monitors). I stood there in the room and respectfully told them I heard what they were saying, but I still had hope and said something like, "God has a higher medical degree than anyone in this room." I was getting tired of the black and white worst-case scenario we got from the doctors. The nurses, however, they prayed with us. They supported our hope. That night, we had the CT scan, and the neurologist confirmed our worst fears.

As they walked us through the next steps, they advised they would do a series of neurological tests on Wednesday night and again twelve hours later on Thursday morning. Wyatt and I both knew Tristan would not want a life less than what he had, neurologically. If God wanted us to care for him that way, we would accept His will. These were conversations we never ever imagined we'd have to have. We'd had the difficult conversations should something happen to one of us, we had a will and were prepared should one of us perish, but not our son. We just could not believe what was happening to us.

Tristan never failed a test in his life. He failed this one. Tristan made the decision we would not have been able to make if the circumstances were one where we would have had to consider taking him off life support. Our hearts sank into our stomachs when they declared him brain dead at 9:48 a.m. on January 19. Eleven years and sixteen days of God's blessing showered upon us. We loved deeply, and so we would grieve deeply.

In the blink of an eye, we went from a perfect Sunday afternoon on a beautiful day in January to this. How would I know that car ride home from the birthday party and our afternoon at home would be the last time I'd speak to Tristan?

We kept asking ourselves, "How did this happen? To *us!*" You hear of tragedies, and you think, "Oh, those poor people." I did. I'd stop and pray and cry for those grieving, but depending on the situation, I was able to carry on with our normal routine while continuing prayers for their peace of mind. I've seen my family and friends do the same. They are forever affected. There is an impact, but nothing like what we were processing.

Immediately following that dreaded Thursday morning, LifeLink of Georgia began working with us. Donating Tristan's organs is what he would have wanted. Tristan had an authentic concern for others and loved to help in all ways possible. We didn't receive the miracle *we* asked for, but through Tristan, we were able to provide a miracle to four others. Tristan saved *four* people's lives. I could see him smiling, eyes looking off to the side a bit, just saying, "That's awesome!" The process to get there was extremely challenging. I was completely naïve to what it took to orchestrate organ donation.

Being a project manager, I could relate to how our LifeLink representative had to juggle multiple balls in the air to make it happen. She worked tirelessly through the night to match organs with individuals in the Southeast *and* time the arrival of all doctors to pick up the organs and get back for transplant surgery with *their* patients. They'd provided me a five-by-seven card to write a message to the doctors and nurses facilitating the surgery as it would be read before starting the surgery. Initially, my response was, "This is it?" I doubled up on each line to fit twice as much as I could. After we'd drafted this for LifeLink, we realized, we'd written his obituary. I can't tell you how many times we said, "What are we doing here? This can't be real." I repeated that about a thousand more times over the course of several weeks and months. The card read:

> Tristan was eleven years old and lived here his whole life. He was *not* your average eleven-year-old! Tristan excelled as an A student and was in the TAG (Talented and Gifted) program. He helped others acclimate in social situations through a group called Circle of Friends. Tristan did this outside of this group, so it was a perfect fit for him.
>
> Tristan was always a leader. He participated in the school play from first to third grade and

got a lead role as Scar in *The Lion King* in fourth grade. Hundreds of parents pulled Tristan's parents aside in amazement of his talent. It was *the* proudest moment of their lives. He was a natural on stage and had been rehearsing to be Captain Hook in *Peter Pan* this February. Tristan started playing basketball when he was four and football when he was eight. He wake boarded, snowboarded, drove go-karts and snowmobiles, and did life *big*.

He was good at anything he tried. The fastest athlete, whether on the field or the court. Tristan was a big brother to Colton, his best bud. Colton will miss his brother so much. Tristan left an impression on *everyone* he came in contact with. He was funny, witty, prayerful, and considerate. He served as an altar boy at our Catholic church and had an amazing relationship with God. His parents will miss him deeply. It was the honor of their lives to be his parents. Tristan is with Jesus in heaven and is smiling about the miracle he is about to provide to the recipients.

LifeLink advised it could be twenty-four to forty-eight hours before they'd have everything in place to conduct the surgery; the average was about twenty-four hours. That was it; we now had a timeline before we'd say our final goodbyes to our precious son. We walked out to our family in that bright waiting room, to the area that had become *our* space with food, drinks, blankets, pillows, and a whole lot of love and support. I couldn't look any of them in the eye. Wyatt explained the diagnosis and that he was gone. So many tears and utter disbelief in that moment. I couldn't look at my mom or my sister. I just couldn't. I glanced at Wyatt's brother, Schuyler, once and saw him begin to break down. Strong Christian people in this space brought to their knees, literally.

Once again, Wyatt's strength carried me through that moment when I couldn't communicate something like that to our family. We began to allow each family member time with Tristan to hold his hand, talk to him, and pray over him as they said goodbye. Wyatt and I spent the next two days in that room, obtaining updates from LifeLink. The school organized all the students to wear orange, Tristan's favorite color, in memory of Tristan and put orange bows up on their marquee out front. We continued to pray for a miracle in our desperation but submitted to God's will.

I went through eleven years of pictures and had about three hundred printed for poster boards my family and friends put together. We began to speak with our pastor's assistant to plan for the readings and songs Tristan would have wanted for his funeral mass. We asked our good friend to write and read words of remembrance—his eulogy. We made appointments at two cemeteries to decide where Tristan would be laid to rest. This is not my life. Wake *up* from this nightmare, Laura. When am I going to wake up?

I had so many conversations with Tristan sitting at his bedside, holding his hand, running my fingers across his chest and through his hair. Sundays in church, we had this thing we'd do sitting next to each other. I'd have my hand on the pew, fingers spread, and he'd "trace" my hand to my pinkie finger, then back to my thumb, then I'd do the same to him. I traced his hand, remembering all the moments that were just ours. Wyatt realized I had a couple other little things I did with just the boys he didn't know of. If we were holding hands walking, one of the boys would squeeze my hand, then I'd squeeze-squeeze, then they'd squeeze-squeeze-squeeze, and on and on. It was our way of saying "I'm right here" without saying a word. As I'd trace Tristan's hands in the hospital and squeeze, I was playing out the movie that was our life together. Although he didn't squeeze back this time, I am thankful for the time we had to hold him and stare at those freckles on his nose and still have hope.

I'd received a wooden cross while we were in the hospital. It's curved to fit perfectly in the palm of your hand. It was given to me *anonymously* by someone who had a child in the ICU, and *they* received it from someone who had had a child in the ICU. When I'm ready and when the situation presents itself, I will pass it along to another parent who needs it. For now, it's provided great comfort and reads "'I am the Lord, your Healer.' (Ex. 5:23). That cross sat in Tristan's hand in the hospital. I kept thinking it was meant for him; the Lord would heal him. The cross was for us. The Lord will heal us. You never heal 100 percent though. How *could* we, with a gaping hole in our hearts that was once filled with the joy Tristan brought to our lives? I sometimes think God *wants* us to have this kind of longing but for the love He can provide. His love is endless and unconditional. We do our best to trust in God, to lean in to His word and grow closer to Him. I ask God to help us get through every single day.

After about four weeks, we received the information about the donor recipients. I had a flurry of emotions reading that letter. I was proud of Tristan for saving others, I was thankful to see young ones getting another chance, but I was angry too. One recipient was sixty-seven years old. My son had to die to save someone that might live another ten years? It's harsh, sorry, but that was my initial thought. I do recognize this recipient is still a person and has loved ones who are happy to have them around. Anger and bitterness pound on my door, but I fight every day to not let them in.

This was our letter to the organ recipients:

> We are hopeful that writing to you will bring healing to us as the parents of an organ donor. We would love to hear from you to know how our son has changed your life.
>
> My name is Laura and my husband is Wyatt, and we have been happily married for almost thirteen years and live in Georgia but we met up in Illinois where all of our family lives. We both still work for the companies we've been with since college (twenty-two years for me and

twenty years for Wyatt). We have two boys, Tristan (in heaven) and Colton, age eight.

Our son was eleven years old when he went to heaven. He was in fifth grade and was a basketball and football player and the lead in the school play for the second year in a row. He had played basketball since he was four and joined football in third grade. Tristan was known for being the fastest one on the field and on the court. He was amazing at everything he tried; a true athlete, a star on stage, a natural-born leader to his brother, friends, and peers. He could capture the attention of any audience, any age. He spoke to adults like an adult, and he went out of his way to help other kids who weren't as comfortable in social settings. He motivated and encouraged his team members to do their best, try their hardest. In addition to football and basketball, Tristan loved snowboarding, wakeboarding, skateboarding, RipStik, roller skating, ice skating, riding go-karts and bikes, swimming, doing flips into the water, going to Six Flags, filling in Mad-Libs on long car rides, taking silly pictures of himself, doing science experiments, taking something apart to learn how it works, or building things out of scrap/recycled materials. He loved reading all the time and could get through a book in a day if given the time. He was a Cub Scout and enjoyed camping with his dad and his brother in the backyard. The boys would get flashlights and sleeping bags and make a big event out of it. He did life *big*.

He was a servant of God and had recently become an altar boy at our Catholic church. Tristan went to religion class on Sundays during the school year and took great pride in receiving the sacraments of the Catholic church (First Reconciliation, First Communion). He'd spent the last two summers at a Christian camp and came home on fire for God and spreading His good news.

We prayed with Tristan and his brother every night, we took them to church on Sundays, we taught them the Ten Commandments, and we tried to live our lives as close to Jesus' as we could. We listened to Christian music on the radio, and the lyrics were a meaningful reminder of what we believe, what we are capable of, what we can endure, and how much we appreciate our blessings. We constantly gave thanks to God for all our blessings and reminded Tristan to give thanks for the talent he had and for how easily it came to him. We know we will see Tristan again when Jesus calls us home.

Tristan was a healthy eleven-year old. "Perfection" comes to mind when we describe him. His accident and death has crippled us with grief. Not seeing him, hugging him, hearing his voice, his laugh, or his witty comments. Not hearing him sing or play with his brother is a loss no parent should have to experience. We are sad, so very sad, but we have trust in God and know He will use our suffering and work through us to bring about good. The emptiness we feel in our hearts and our home is unbearable at times.

We know Tristan would not have had it any other way, and if asked about organ donation, he would have said, "Absolutely. It's what God would want." Knowing Tristan's gift is *your* miracle brings a little help as we try to comprehend or understand what has happened. The only thing we can reconcile is Tristan fulfilled his purpose in life in a very short period of time. The impact he had on many lives of his family, neighbors, friends, and even strangers is compelling. God needed Tristan for His army. Everyone who knew Tristan understands that.

Tristan used to ask to pay for the car behind us if we went through the drive-through at Chick-fil-A or Starbucks. Since his passing, we've handed out thousands of orange "Pay It Forward" cards to remember Tristan's love of random acts of kindness. We know he is smiling every time someone gets to the window to find out their coffee or meal is free today. He was so thoughtful, and he saw things unlike other eleven-year-olds (even though he was a typical eleven-year-old a *lot* of the time). Tristan wore a shirt (*all* the time) he had received from camp that said *"HOPE: more than meets the eye, 2 Corinthians 4:18."* This Bible verse tells us what we see here on earth is temporary, but what is unseen is eternal. Our faith allows us to see our eternity with God much more clearly. We would love to hear about your path in life and how it has been changed by the gift provided through Tristan's organ donation.

I did hear from two of the four donor recipients. It's difficult. I want them to know how much we're struggling. Why? What good does that do? Nothing. I can recognize these negative emotions so easily now—the jealousy, envy, anger, all driven by the evil one. When I question if what I'm feeling or thinking is coming from me, from God, or the evil one, it's easier to discern now. I see right through the devil's pathetic ways. God did not create us for anger or jealousy. It does not matter how sad I am, I will never ever give up on my belief in Christ. I tell the devil, the worst has already been done to me, and I still trust, I still believe, I still hope.

> Blessed be the God and Father of our Lord Jesus Christ, who in his great mercy he has given us new birth to a living hope through the resurrection of Jesus Christ from the dead, to an inheritance that is imperishable, undefiled and unfading, kept in heaven for you who by the power of God are safeguarded through faith, to a salvation that is ready to be revealed in the final time. In this you rejoice, although now, for a little while you may have to suffer through various trials. (1 Pet. 1:3–6, NAB)

Tristan, My Baby Doll

Tristan, being the firstborn, would constantly amaze us. He was just good at *everything* he tried. He started playing basketball when he was four and played every winter. He tried baseball one season and wasn't asking to do it again, so we stuck to basketball in the winter and swimming lessons every summer. By the end of second grade, he said he wanted to join football. Practice started in late July 2014 just before third grade, with conditioning before teams were picked. It was a defining season for us. Tristan was *fast*—really fast. Get him the ball, and he's *gone!* I cannot say enough good things about his coach that year. His son became a good friend of Tristan's, and we were always thankful for the one-on-one time Coach offered Tristan to become a better player. There are so many memories after eleven beautiful years with Tristan, but the ones within the last few years stand out. That makes sense. I don't get upset seeing pictures of him as a baby or a toddler. It's seeing pictures of the Tristan I loved before Jesus brought him home—that's the Tristan I miss so much.

When Tristan was gearing up for fourth grade, he went out for football again. He was drafted to another team, and we had another fabulous season although it was hard not to be with his coach again. Tristan enjoyed meeting new kids and new coaches, and some of them stood out and made a real impact on Tristan and his team-mates. I loved the camaraderie of rooting for our boys with the other parents at games. I'd envisioned myself going to high school games and being the rowdy, passionate parents cheering on our boys.

In late fall 2015 (fourth grade), Tristan decided he wanted to try out for a *lead* role in the school play. They were putting on *The Lion King*. I'd advised him leads typically went to fifth graders, but go for it. Let me just say, the school plays at our elementary school rivaled some high school productions. Parent volunteers make it an amazing drama club program. If I wasn't working, I would have loved to spend more time volunteering to help them learn songs, dances, and lines. Such a healthy extracurricular outlet.

Tristan and I spent a few nights practicing different audition songs and landed on "Crazy Little Thing Called Love" by Queen. He had to sing it a cappella and knocked the audition out of the park. I have a video of him practicing in our kitchen after football practice one night. I am so thankful for that video and so many others. He landed the lead role of Scar. We could not believe it. I have great memories of practicing lines with him and singing songs, but I never watched him *at* play practice. I cried a little when I saw him on stage for the first time. Wyatt and I could not believe he had the God-given talent to be so confident on stage, speak in an English accent the whole time, *and* sing the way he did! What! Tristan was always smart and talented when it came to school and sports, but performing arts too? Was there anything he couldn't do? Like I said, he was good at everything he tried.

What a proud moment for him. Signing autographs after the show and taking pictures. What a proud moment for us! I've never had so many parents come up to me to tell me how amazing my son was. They'd ask, "Did you know he could sing and perform like that?" Truth was, we knew Tristan could be good at anything, but we had no idea. He stole the show. He was on top of the world after three nights of performances. I was on cloud nine; so proud to be "Tristan's Mom." How did I go from *"Hey, you're Tristan's Mom!"* to *"Oh* (long pause) *you're Tristan's Mom?"* in the span of a year?

Wyatt coached a couple of Tristan's basketball seasons, but work travel had limited his ability to coach in 2016. There were a few families that did basketball year after year like we did. One family in particular that we knew from our daycare became good friends of ours. Wyatt and the other dad had coached basketball together one year and enjoyed it, so Wyatt was his assistant coach again for the winter 2016 season. Our friend is an amazing coach and father to his three kids; his oldest son was a good bud of Tristan's. Those two, man, they ran the show on the basketball court. They had a great time together.

We didn't have the opportunity to finish that last season. There was a game that Thursday night; they gave Tristan the first two points. I heard our dear friend and coach cried through the game. We won, so I know Tristan was high-fiving in heaven. He was so passionate about the sport, and I know he and Wyatt had such a strong relationship with basketball in the middle of it. They shot so many baskets on our driveway; it was one of many bonding moments they had. Wyatt is heartbroken over not being able to watch Tristan wow the middle school, high school, and college teams that he would have played on. We feel the same about all of Tristan's talents. The world went dim when Tristan went home to be with Jesus, but his light shines bright in heaven.

Tristan and I had recent conversations about heaven before his accident. One night, before bed, he asked me what I thought heaven was like. We talked about what the Bible says and whether one person's heaven is different than another? Would we have a house? The Bible speaks of mansions! If so, could one window face the mountains with snow on them and another face the beach? Tristan loved both seasons. He knew I despised cold weather, but I told him in heaven, I could enjoy snow and not be cold. We talked about people you'd see in heaven—our grandparents who had gone before us, ancestors we didn't know, the disciples and saints! He'd asked me one day after school if I was afraid to die. I told him flat out, "No, I know where I'm going, and I am not afraid. It will be wonderful."

I've often pictured my reunion with Jesus, hand stretched out, welcoming me, and there's Tristan running toward me, in his green HOPE shirt. He says, "Mom, you're here! You're not going to believe this place. Wait till I show you…"

Faith, Hope, Love

So how *does* one even get through a tragedy like this? My answer: *faith*. And the key word is *through*. I know we will not be stuck in this valley forever. God *will* bring us through it.

My faith grew exponentially over the last eleven years, and I know God provided me the foundation I needed to endure this trial. He knows our path before it happens, and although He's given us free will out of love for us, He still knows the future. He saw the path this could have taken. If Tristan hadn't had the accident at all, we'd be going about our day, maybe a little complacent about our relationship with Christ. If Tristan had been saved, we'd have had a path of recovery and then back to our normal routine eventually. The path He chose has the most impact on us, on His followers, and on those who don't yet know Him well.

I'd felt a pull toward a stronger relationship with God during our Pre-Cana sessions the summer of 2004. In the Catholic church, Pre-Cana is the preparation prior to the sacrament of marriage. We met weekly with a couple from our church, and they opened my eyes to music and books that would *encourage* my faith journey, coaching us to rely on prayer and turn away from that which could serve as a temptation to worldly things in lieu of living every day for God. My eyes were further opened after a CRHP retreat where I learned *everyone has a story*.

In May 2006, when Tristan was only four months old, I attended CRHP (pronounced "Chirp"; Christ Renews His Parish). It catapulted my faith in God. No longer could I judge a book by its cover. Everyone had something that was either going on or *had* gone on in their lives that could not be seen on the outside. The strength of women who had overcome trials in their lives by faith was encouraging, and I came home on fire for God. Tristan felt the same way when he came home from WinShape Camp two summers in a row. I was so thankful he felt that way and shared our love of God so passionately.

In the weeks after the retreat, I remained with the group to discern my calling to participate in hosting the *next* retreat. I took on what felt like the biggest role as "facilitator." I am a project manager by nature and by trade, so although I had a full-time job and a four-month old, I felt called to volunteer for this position that would organize the whole retreat and then execute the next weekend in six months. My time spent with the women from *my* retreat and then the women on the next one was so powerful and so meaningful to me. I started listening to a Christian radio station, and the lyrics were scripture and filled me with such joy, celebrating the praise and worship of God and comfort of His constant presence. I began going to confession regularly. I know for a fact my family saw a change in me and how close I had come to know Jesus, Scripture, and how strongly I relied on my faith during difficult times. Over the years, I encouraged others to do the same. In times of need, pray. In good times, give thanks. God is good all the time, and all the time, God is good.

I joined our children's liturgy team and began working with the kids in our parish to bring a simpler form of the mass to them. At first, I was nervous to do my own homily but then I loved it. I'd become comfortable with public speaking through my career, and this was even easier. They were just kids! I loved sharing the good news with them and had even more fun with it when Tristan was old enough to start attending, then Colton. When both boys were able to help carry the banner down the aisle and participate in the mass, I had an even bigger smile on my face.

For many years, my trials came in the form of stress from work or the health of our parents. Of late, it was the shuffle to manage my job and the boys both in sports while Wyatt was traveling. I give a lot of credit to single moms and dads. In May of 2013, I was promoted to manage the team I'd been a part of for several years. Achieving a career goal set nearly fifteen years prior was a big deal for me, and I was elated. Although it was a little awkward to be a team member and then the manager of that team, it was a smooth transition, and I knew the type of manager I wanted to be. I used my position to motivate and inspire at every opportunity possible. I made the team aware my priorities were God-family-work. I was never shy about my faith and would speak openly to them about it. As I heard stories of people falling on hard times through personal relationships or articles I'd read, I used it as a means to ensure the team was taking care of themselves, eating right, exercising, getting enough sleep, and doing what made them happy.

The job was stressful. I'd done it and been in their shoes, so I knew firsthand what they were going through with demanding customers and tight timelines. Many of us averaged ten- to twelve-hour days just to stay afloat. A large part of my role as manager was talking them off the ledge and reprioritizing what they had on their plate. Lots and lots of pep talks.

I had made a point to practice what I preach and really started to abide by boundaries I'd set. Workout at least three times a week, carve out the time for it, block time for lunch, no calls after five o'clock in the afternoon. That last one was big! I was doing much better, shutting down right at five to go pick up the boys from their after-school program, get home, make dinner, watch thirty minutes of television, read with them, say prayers, go to bed, wake up, and repeat. At the end of 2016, I'd earned another promotion to director and was really excited about it. I was going to eventually promote one of my employees to take my place and work on bigger, more complex projects. This promotion was a blessing in disguise. While in the hospital, just a month or so after my promotion, my right-hand gal stepped up, and I knew she had me covered. I texted my boss and told him I didn't know if I could ever return to work if we lost Tristan. I saw my whole life slipping away.

Wyatt and I came home from the hospital on Saturday (two days after they'd pronounced Tristan brain dead). It started raining Friday, and the flights getting into Atlanta delayed some of the doctors coming in for the organ donation surgery. The surgery was bumped from Friday night to four in the morning Saturday and then bumped again to early Saturday afternoon. Each time, it was a gut punch as we just wanted closure. We were planning a funeral and friends were saying how sorry they were, but I was still holding his hand, warm in my grip. Wyatt and I would take turns lying next to him in the hospital bed. Finally, around noon on Saturday, they told us it was time.

Every night, before bed, we prayed with the boys. "Now I lay me, down to sleep." We prayed that prayer one last time over Tristan before we said our final goodbye. Watching them wheel him away wearing Wyatt's orange University of Illinois hat was a separation I never thought I'd have to deal with. I think back to the first day I dropped him off at daycare, only twelve weeks old, the first day I put him on the school bus for kindergarten, the first time I dropped him off at overnight summer camp for a week... For as much as I had anxiety about being away from him at *those* times, this was deeper and hurt more than words can express. The double doors of the ICU opened, and we walked out. Our family met us there, and we made our way to the parking garage. It was pouring rain. The gray skies matched our emotions, and we were now in the eye of the storm.

Once we got home, I couldn't get out of the car after Wyatt pulled into the garage. There were people in my kitchen and neighbors who had brought food, fresh flowers, and boxes of tissues. I kept my head down and went straight up to bed and slept. I hadn't slept in days and was emotionally and physically exhausted. Sitting there in my bed, I remember the pain that washed over me. I put the canvas we'd made the first night in the hospital, the boys' handprints, on the shelf in my room. I thought, if I wake up and see it, I'll know it's real; if it's not there, I'll know it was just a horrible nightmare. I keep waking up, and it's still there. I tell myself I want to die. I don't want to be here. Lord, please, take us back or take us home.

I came downstairs, and Tristan's assistant football coach was sitting on our couch. Family was there, and I tried to eat. The next day, we had to visit the funeral home and two cemeteries. We could not believe what we were doing. Picking out a coffin and an outfit to bury him in? I was in a nightmare—a living hell. The wake was on Tuesday. Wyatt and I stood for four hours straight, greeting friends, family, neighbors, coworkers, and even strangers. We aren't quite sure how we got through that evening. It felt like a presentation I just had to get through. Keep your composure, Laura. Be strong. I was so emotionally distraught inside but staying strong on the outside. The last thing I wanted to do was hug one more person, but I was polite. They were grieving too.

We sat with our pastor for a bit after the wake. People were still cleaning up. Neighbors had supplied food. The number of plants and flowers was overwhelming. I asked to keep the plants but sent the flowers to a local retirement home. As we approached our neighborhood, I noticed someone on the sidewalk outside our subdivision and then I caught the lights. The street leading up to our house and our driveway was lined with luminaries, and many neighbors were just there, standing outside on a cold night welcoming us home from a terrible day.

It was like nothing I'd ever seen and like nothing I've ever felt from our friends and neighbors. I'm going on record to state they are the *best* set of neighbors anyone could ever ask for. In the next coming weeks and months, they surrounded us with love, sympathy, and food—lots of food. My one neighbor said, "We just don't know what to do but feed you." That works. When you don't know what to say, it's okay to say, "I don't have the words. Here's a casserole." I could probably publish a cookbook of the many meals we received and are ever so grateful for.

When I was in the hospital, I started talking about doing a Pay It Forward card in the waiting room area we'd claimed for our family. I wanted something that would keep Tristan's name and memory alive; something that would continue to spread kindness in his spirit. Tristan had often asked to pay for the car behind us if we went through the drive-through at Chick-fil-A. I used to joke, "What if that family has six kids? The bill could be huge?" That was Tristan though; he thought it would be so cool to surprise them with a free meal.

One of the many people who were helping to execute the numerous tasks needed in forty-eight hours had cards printed so they were available at the wake and the funeral. We handed out thousands. Others printed more on their own. I've had a few strangers contact me via Facebook Messenger, telling me they received a free meal or coffee in honor of Tristan. He's smiling over every random act of kindness that's taken place, and we will continue it for as long as we live. I always told the boys we must be mindful of our thoughts, actions, and words; let it always be for the glory of God.

Tristan, I wish we had paid it forward a hundred times when you were here with us. Your spirit is with me every time I hand the cashier that orange card, asking them to let the person behind me know theirs is free today. My local Starbucks and Chick-fil-A get the majority of my Pay It Forward cards. I love when I get a cashier who says, "Oh, I know what to do with this!" Then there are the cashiers who can't *believe* I'd pay for a stranger's coffee. "Really? That is so sweet!" I left stacks of cards at our daycare to hand out to parents and dropped off cards at a local Catholic gift store. The elementary school still has Tristan's picture and a stack of Pay it Forward cards at the front desk.

After the funeral, our church provided lunch for the hundreds of people who attended the mass. The church was full, like it is on Christmas or Easter. Our long-time friend spoke eloquently about Tristan's life and service to God and others. I kept my eyes toward the floor and held onto Colton's hand as we walked out behind the casket that afternoon. We stood for another two hours, greeting people, some we had seen the night before, others offering their condolences for the first time. We maintained our composure again, feeling like it was more of an out-of-body experience. When Wyatt's boss stepped up, I knew we couldn't hold it in. Tears flowed hard. Wyatt's boss and owner of the company he's worked for since he graduated from college flew in from LA.

It wasn't just his presence that set us off; it was *his* Pay It Forward that we would never forget. He'd contacted the hospital admissions office to cover our hospital bills. Additionally, he paid for all the hotel rooms for family who had come in for the funeral and for the actual funeral. It was an unbelievable act of generosity. He treated us like family, and Wyatt has always felt like a loyal brother to him. This was not a surprise. This is how he runs his company—employees are family. It is the one thing I've talked about when people ask what Wyatt does for a living. The culture of this company is like none other. None. Our gratitude is endless.

We had family staying with us for six weeks straight. My mom left, my sister-in-law came in, she left, my in-laws came down, they left, my brother-in-law came in. They went to the grocery store, did laundry, and helped with dinner—anything we needed. I didn't talk much those first few weeks, only to Wyatt and Colton. For the first week after the funeral, Wyatt and I would get Colton to school and go back to bed until noon. We eventually started to come downstairs around ten, and over the following weeks, we were able to stay downstairs after Colton got on the bus at seven.

I went back to work six weeks after the funeral. I made sure my right-hand gal was promoted while I was out on bereavement leave, and I came back with a clean slate but zero motivation to do anything. Being creative and innovative seemed impossible. My boss respectfully only gave me what I asked for, and every week or two, I'd ask for more. I had to stay busy, but even when I *was* busy, I could barely focus. I'd put my gym membership on hold but started to get out walking and then got back to jogging. My neighbor became a strong support system, listening to me on bad days, coaching me on my running form, motivating me to keep up with the exercise (especially since I was against antidepressants), and checking in on me *all* the time. She really saved me. She has a heart of gold, and I am forever grateful.

Every day, there would be several cards in the mail, and after three months, we would still receive a card or two a week. Every week, for nearly six months, someone would bring dinner or lunch or drop off flowers or a necklace or a journal. Such thoughtfulness from our community at a time when no one knew what to say or do. Let me tell you, if you ever have to comfort someone who has gone through a loss, don't go silent. Not hearing from people you thought you'd hear from was surprising to me. I felt awful for the times I might not have been there for someone else when they expected *me* to be a comfort or support to them. It takes no effort to text when you are too afraid to call.

I was in some kind of autopilot mode to get through the wake and the funeral. I was still in shock. We had all these people over after the funeral and it felt like one of our parties with kids playing outside, adults having drinks, food on the counter. I just kept moving on auto-pilot playing hostess. People kept hugging me and I was to the point where I wanted to scream "stop touching me!" At times they were upset and I knew I could not be the one to console; I would just stand there frozen and silent. I don't think I could tell you who was there or how long they were there. Eventually when there were just a few left I was sitting on the couch unable to keep my eyes open. My mom finally said, "She needs to go to bed" and that was everyone's cue to skedaddle. Weeks went by and then months, and everyone's life was moving forward but ours was still completely broken in pieces on the floor.

Some of our support team would offer different resources as outlets to help our grieving process. We received Bible verses, reference to websites, and a lot of books. Two books I read specifically helped me. The first one we started reading right after the funeral called *Through the Eyes of a Lion* by Levi Lusko. One of our nurses sent it. The author is a pastor up in Montana who lost his second-born daughter, Lenya. His words articulated how we felt, yet here he was, able to carry on and even encourage others? We read his book to each other while lying in bed those mornings until noon. The other book that spoke to me was *Rare Bird* by Anna Whiston-Donaldson. I felt such a connection to the author. I e-mailed her, and she e-mailed me back the next day! Bereaved mothers' club.

If we weren't reading, we were listening to preachers we enjoyed, like Dr. Michael Youssef, Alastair Begg, and Ravi Zacharias. I downloaded the app for Levi Lusko's Fresh Life Church and listened to at least one of his Sunday sermons per day. Sometimes his message was the only thing that got me out of bed. I started to share his book and app with anyone who asked how I was doing. Months later, I'd come across a website, LightSource Today, and got daily e-mails containing five or so videos of sermons. I came to enjoy listening to James MacDonald, Sheila Walsh, Jeff Schreve, and Rick Warren. If I was struggling, I'd cue up one of their sermons, and it brought me peace. I'd listen to them when I woke up way before my alarm was set to go off or while having a cup of coffee. They were there for me when I was taking a long walk or trying to fall asleep. Everyone kept asking me if I was seeing someone (a doctor) regularly. I'd say no. I was reading the Bible and listening to people speak about the Bible. It contains all I need.

Some friends and acquaintances shared that our experience had brought them back to a life of prayer or had started a new path for them. Wyatt and I asked over and over again at the wake and the funeral reception for people to *pray*, trust God, and, more importantly, pray with their children.

I'd always kept a copy of *Jesus Calling* on my desk in my office. It is crazy how, so many days, my reaction to the devotional would be, "How could that be the message today!?" It would match up with what I was going through at work or elsewhere, and I'd do my best to stay in communication with God. I gave thanks every morning before I got out of bed, I gave thanks throughout the day for glimpses of God's glory, and I prayed when I needed Him. After Tristan's funeral, I started diving into Scripture; I'd reference the ones on each page of my *Jesus Calling* book or the one the preacher was giving his sermon on looking for answers. I was like a sponge; I couldn't get enough. I couldn't find answers, but I could find *hope*. I kept hearing, "Just trust me," even though I'd fight it.

Tristan was buried in his camp WinShape HOPE shirt. When we looked through pictures of him from 2015–2017, he had it on all the time. That one and the red Blaze shirt from camp, which signified what "squad" he belonged to. While in the hospital, we decided in lieu of flowers, we wanted any donations to go to a Tristan Schupbach Memorial Fund so we could send other boys to camp.

WinShape Camps was established in 1985 by the Cathy family (founders of Chick-fil-A restaurants) in Mount Berry, Georgia, to provide a camp experience that would enable campers to sharpen their character, deepen their Christian faith, and grow in their relationships with others. Every thank you card I sent following a donation received a Pay It Forward card.

We met with the folks at Chick-fil-A's gorgeous campus in Atlanta at the end of February, one month after the funeral. We were still pretty raw, and our emotions were out on the table as we talked about the fund and how it would be used in the summer of 2017 and ongoing. I was so very impressed with the team we worked with and with Chick-fil-A corporate overall. I've always loved how they ran their company, but being there, it felt like being at church! I felt a calm come over me while we were visiting. They donated HOPE shirts leftover from the 2015 camp, so we could sell them and put the proceeds right back into the fund.

We hope to keep the fund going for many years to come. Our *hope* is that scholarship recipients of the Tristan Schupbach Memorial Fund can see that which is unseen: "For what we see today is temporary, but what is unseen is eternal" (2 Cor. 4:18). Donations from the funeral were substantial, and we were able to send eight boys to camp for the 2017 summer sessions! We hope it helps to build or further a child's relationship with God. Wyatt and I feel drawn to a closer relationship with God ourselves, longing for heaven, and will spread the Word of God for the sake of the salvation of others. Fill the lifeboats!

In August, a neighbor organized a bake sale through Little Helpers of Atlanta tagging it as "Baking It Forward for Tristan." Every goodie had an orange heart with a Bible verse or inspirational quote. Many of our friends donated baked goods or stopped by to shop, and the support was tremendous. We raised half of the money we would need to send eight more kids to camp in the summer of 2018! Unbelievable! It was apparent Tristan had a true impact on the community.

Orange Moments

While we were in the hospital, Wyatt reminded me of a dream he'd had the week prior. He was at a funeral, at a grave site. Weeks earlier, I'd had a premonition; it felt like a bad daydream where someone told me Tristan was gone. I was watching a movie where the mom had lost one of two sons, and my mind started to wander. When I snapped out of it, I was crying. What's odd is for years, I'd felt I was going to live with a deep, deep sadness.

I was convinced this sadness was Wyatt. *Would he leave me? Cheat on me? Would God take him from me?* Was it just a fear of abandonment being a child of divorce? It didn't just feel like waiting for the other shoe to drop; it felt like it was something I *knew* was going to be in my future.

In the year before Tristan's accident and death, I had watched coworkers and friends deal with grief. A dear friend of mine experienced a terrible accident leaving his wife paralyzed from the neck down. She joined Tristan in heaven only a few months after him. A coworker lost his twenty-year-old daughter in a drowning accident, then months later, an employee of mine lost his seven-month-old son to SIDS. *Was that God's way of preparing me? Exposing me to these awful situations?* We are exposed to stories like this all the time, but these were too close.

In the two years prior to Tristan's accident, our elementary school lost two precious boys. I'd attended a balloon release for one of them, and my heart just broke for the boy's mother. I remember saying "Thank you, God" that my boys were safe, yet here I was, in her shoes. I became friends with the other mom, my kindred spirit, as I joined a group I never wanted to be a part of. Until I am granted entry into God's kingdom, I will never know whether these incidents were preparation for my circumstances. My faith was the only "preparation" I had to truly endure this.

So let me explain an *Orange Moment*. Tristan's favorite color was orange, so an orange moment, as I started to call them, were times where something happened that reminded me of Tristan and gave me hope. Some were small, simple things; others were powerful, unexplained incidents.

On the Wednesday we were in the hospital, friends had gone by the house to get clothes and such to bring to us. Our neighbors were in and out of the house helping to put our bathroom back together in working order. They went and got the vanity out of the dumpster that Wyatt and Tristan had carried the day of his accident when we thought it was the last time we'd need it. They not only put the bathroom back together; they cleaned the house of all the dust from the tile Wyatt had been ripping up! They are all just too good to us.

Here's the strange thing: one friend indicated there had been a bird in the house. We've never had a bird in our house. After we were home, we experienced two more birds in the house, all within two weeks of his accident. The third time, I closed a door behind me, containing our flying friend, knowing I could open an *outside* patio door to let it out. The bird never flew. It calmly hopped around the room toward me until I was right in front of it, asking, "Are you okay?" I'm talking to a bird. It hopped over the threshold onto the patio, hopped a little further, turned back as if to look at me, and then finally flew off.

I wondered if that was a sign of sorts but was a bit of a skeptic. We have not had a bird in the house since and still have no explanation for how they got into the house. We never found an open window; maybe it flew into the fireplace, but there was no proof of an access point. A friend from church later told me there is significance with the number three. "The Father, the Son, and the Holy Ghost visited you."

I couldn't make it to church the Sunday after we got home from the hospital, but we did go back the Sunday *after* the funeral. That was rough. We sat in the same pew every Sunday, the four of us. Sitting there, just the three of us felt even more empty than it did being at home without him in his room. In the pew in front of us was an orange crayon. I pointed to it, and Colton said, "That reminds me of Tristan!"

A week after the funeral, I started going to the Tuesday afternoon play rehearsals to be with Colton. I wasn't working, so it gave me a reason to shower and get out of the house. Wyatt dove into other projects, and it was only an hour rehearsal. I continued to help out, steering clear of the boy who would fill Tristan's role as Captain Hook in Peter Pan. I was heartbroken he didn't have the opportunity to wow the audience with this performance, although this would be one of several performances, games, presentations, and the like that we'd feel the loss.

When the play came around, I was helping in the green room to keep Colton's pirate crew preoccupied until their time came to go on stage. The play ran for three nights. Wyatt and I watched the first half of the play to see Colton's scene and ducked out before Captain Hook came on. The drama club graciously allowed us to sit in a dark, quiet sound booth all by ourselves to watch. The thoughtfulness of those around us just continued to pour out. At the start of the play, all the fifth graders came out with orange bandanas on to dedicate this play "to our friend, Tristan." So touching. Emotions were all over the place. That should be him up there! Why did this have to happen to *our* son? Why Tristan? Why the most amazing kid in the world... The only explanation I have is God needed him, and by God's grace, we *will* see him again. *Trust me, Laura.*

A few weeks into spring baseball practice, Colton and I stayed late after a practice to run his remote control cars in the field. I'd kept an eye out as people we were walking on the sidewalk behind our field. As we packed up to leave, we noticed an orange bandana, standing up like a dinner napkin does when you get to the table. I looked around, and there was no one in sight. Still skeptical, I started to wonder, was that placed here to remind us of Tristan?

One of the many times I was in his room, I came across an art folder he'd made by stapling the sides and bottom of the sheets together. I didn't recall seeing it before and the artwork inside was nothing particularly special, but it was the *outside* of the folder that stopped me in my tracks. There were three faces drawn, two big faces on the top and one smaller face below, and the words "I will watch over you" written by Tristan. Three faces. Not the four of us; the three of us.

I replay the day of his accident over and over. That day, a neighbor had noticed Tristan about to skateboard down our street, which slopes down. He had a helmet on, but our neighbor said, "Does your dad know you're about to do that?" Tristan said yes. We'd made a pact with our neighbors years ago. It takes a village, and we watch out for each other's kids all the time. We'd make sure they didn't go running into the street to get a ball; we'd make sure they obeyed the rules regardless of whose house they were at. As our neighbor walked away that day, Tristan heard him say under his breath, "That kid's gonna kill himself one day." It's just something you say, and Tristan was a risk taker.

Tristan told me what he said, and I said, "It's okay. He didn't mean anything. He's just watching out for you."

In that moment, could I have saved him? Should I have said something different? Would my words in that moment give us a different outcome? Who would have ever known that in just a few hours from that conversation, my husband would be doing CPR.

We are caring and careful parents, but we were not so crazy overprotective that we didn't let them have fun. But it makes me so angry. I put them through years of swimming lessons to make sure they'd never drown. I had boundaries so no one went into the street; I had rules so they didn't leave our yard without permission. I taught them right from wrong, good from bad, safe from dangerous, and *every* single day, I said, "Make good choices." Like Wyatt's dream and my premonition, it just felt like another warning.

The one sign I couldn't ignore came nearly three months after his accident. Spring break rolled around, and we originally had a trip planned to Orlando for three nights, but neither of us wanted to go. We couldn't go. Too many memories of the time we took the boys to Disney (twice) and the time just two years ago when we took them to Universal Studios, my favorite family vacation. We just loved the Harry Potter rides, the train, Diagon Alley, butterbeer, all of it. Colton was still too small for some rides so maybe it wasn't *his* favorite trip, but I have such wonderful memories.

I called and had our 2017 spring break plans switched to head to Myrtle Beach as we'd never been there. On the beach, I was pacing back and forth while Colton was in the water playing. I said, "Lord, if I could find a heart-shaped shell or stone, I'd *know* you've heard me."

Within the hour, Colton walked up and said, "Mom, look! What does this look like?"

I said, "Well, that looks like a heart!"

He said "That's what I thought! It reminded me of Tristan."

I had said the prayer silently and *never* told him or Wyatt that I'd prayed it. It was a pretty *specific* prayer too. *Okay, okay, so you hear me.* I still struggled with how this could be our life. Wyatt would just shake his head left to right all the time, and I knew he was thinking, "This cannot be real. This can't be our life." God makes no mistakes, so I know the path we are on is one of His doing and it has purpose. We may not see that until we meet Him face to face, but it's there. I just want to understand so bad.

God is at work, and His timeline is never the same as ours. I want answers now, and believe me, I've had it out with God. I have yelled and screamed and begged for Him to take us back in time, over and over and over. "You're God. Bend time, and take us back. Let us keep this new perspective, but take us back!" Take us back to Thanksgiving or to Christmas in Illinois or our snowmobiling trip up in the north woods of Wisconsin at New Year's Eve or the afternoon of January 15 or in the hospital—just take us back. I've asked God why so many times; I know He's got to think it's getting old. You, again? Didn't I tell you to trust me? Stop asking why. One of the books I read, *Safe in the Arms of God*, said to start asking "What now?" so I shifted my focus. How can I serve you better, Lord? What wasn't I doing before that I can do more of or do differently or better *now*?

Reading became a distraction for me. An acquaintance had recommended the book *Imagine Heaven* by John Burke. I Googled it and found a series of videos and started watching them. I found great peace in hearing stories of near-death experiences and the consistencies across the stories speaking of the abundance of love and peace. Each of them spoke to the "light"—a light that wasn't like sunlight you can't look into but more like brilliance, a light that contained a love you could feel. I know Tristan recognized Jesus the minute he saw Him. I picture Tristan, a little starstruck when he was in His presence. "Oh my gosh, it's *you!* You're Jesus!" We often sang the song "I Can Only Imagine" by MercyMe in the car and talked about what our first reaction would be when we came face to face with Jesus one day.

We talked about whether we'd run to Him in one of those hugs where you nearly knock someone over in excitement of seeing them or fall to our knees, so thankful to be in His presence? I can see Tristan doing a combination of both, uncontrolled excitement, literally bouncing, and then a realization to bow down out of respect. I know Tristan reached the threshold of heaven and never looked back. Why would you? Those who claim they have been there indicate they didn't want to leave. For those who have been sent back, it was to fulfill a purpose. Tristan fulfilled his purpose in only eleven years. Whether his purpose was wrapped up in the impact he had on us, our family, his friends, or *all* of us, he made an impact. As our story reached the community and we had Pay It Forward cards out there, his life had a further impact on people who had never met him but came to know how special he was.

After reading that book, I thought about heaven a lot. I wanted to see heaven, to see that Tristan was there, enjoying God's kingdom, fulfilling his new role without a sense of time like we have here on earth. I had a dream in September, and it was one of those powerful dreams you can't shake. Up until this point, I'd only had a few dreams where I saw Tristan. In each dream, I'd see him, and I'd frantically say, "You're *here!* Don't move. Stay right there!" Or I'd hug him and then the dream was over too soon. This particular dream I had was more. I remembered so much of it, and I could remember texture and color and sensations like no other dream.

Cue the dream sequence sounds. Wyatt and I were in a city and explaining that Tristan had been gone for five weeks (it had been nine months, so I didn't know what the reference to five weeks meant). A small group of people took us out on a boat and brought us to a part of the lake where we stopped. A Loch Ness monster (leviathan) was in the water, and we all knew this was Tristan's Loch Ness monster. He asked me to climb on. I jumped out of the boat into the water and climbed up onto its back. At no point did I balk at the fact that the Loch Ness monster was *talking* to me. The base of its body was very wide. My arms stretched out didn't reach either side, but I could feel the dark, smooth, tough skin like that of a seal or a whale. He said, "Hold on," and I felt it propel us through the water with the flip of his back legs. I remember the sensation of going very fast across the lake, almost like flying, and the water was perfectly calm all around us. He asked me, "Why do you want to find Tristan so bad?"

I said, "I'm his mother, and I need to know where he is and if he's okay."

We came to an island, and as we approached, I could see all these children bustling about. Their ages ranged from about eight to eighteen, and they were all busy moving about in small groups. But they were dedicated and working. As we came to the shore of this island, there wasn't a deep beach. The tree line was only about fifteen to twenty feet away, and I looked up and saw Tristan in a group of about four kids his age. He was wearing his red Blaze shirt from camp. When I saw him, I told the Loch Ness monster, "There he is! He's here!" I had an overwhelming sense of relief; one I had not felt in months. Tristan looked at me and then seemed like he had to finish his conversation quickly before excusing himself from the group. I hugged him on the shoreline there. A good long hug. I made an observation to the Loch Ness monster and said, "They aren't gathering food or logs?"

I recognized that they weren't trying to survive; they were thriving. These kids were busy but they weren't *stuck* on this deserted island. Next, there were five speedboats lined up to my left, and as the speedboats began to pull away from the shore, kids popped up on wakeboards, one row, then another row, like a ski show! Then in the third row, kids had other kids on their shoulders. Tristan was on the second boat in the third row and had a girl on his shoulders, and they were *all* smiling and laughing. It felt like that was the little glimpse of heaven I'd asked God to show me. At no time during the dream did I expect Tristan would be coming back with me. It was like I understood this is where he would stay and he was alright; he was more than alright.

At nine months out, I attended a Christian retreat in the hopes that I may hear God with a booming voice guiding me to an opportunity that helps answer *why* He allowed this to happen to us. The retreat included all walks of life, and I realized bad stuff happens to a *lot* of people. So maybe I didn't get a booming voice, but I did get *something*.

When I arrived, I'd told myself, "No one is going through the level of pain I am. I am carrying the *heaviest* cross of all." *How naïve of me.* There is something about fellowship among women that just allows you to let it all out, especially when you're with kindred spirits.

My husband says, "Wow, women, you need to talk so much more than men."

True statement; it's therapeutic. Perspective is what allows us to see the world in a different light, and I received perspective from the women that weekend.

Get this, my cross is pretty heavy, *but* it may not be the heaviest of all. The weekend allowed me to see and accept gifts God has given me that can be used for good within our circumstances. I am strong, stronger than I thought; strong enough to speak about what's happened to me, to witness to others and bring them to a life with Christ and keep walking in faith despite our pain. I learned that being shackled with grief is just as hard as being shackled by an addiction or an abusive past. Suffering hurts no matter what form it comes in. Each of us is or has been in a valley, and a valley is a valley is a valley. Thing about valleys or deep holes is you can't always see your way out, or so I thought. Turns out we have the seeds to grow from the pain; it's just that those seeds need to be covered in dirt and darkness before they'll sprout. I'm in the darkness, and I still struggle to see my way out of this valley.

In my envy, I compared myself to other women who were already out of *their* valley. I said, "See, they're okay now. I'll *never* be okay." The pain is like a fog that disorients me; the darkness keeps me from seeing the light I know is ahead. That's how pain and depression work. That's how the devil works. He loves to revel in our despair. Hope kills the devil's plans though, so—*ha!*—Jesus wins again, I'm on His side. I would do my best to replace my thoughts by repeating, "God created heaven and earth. He sent his Son to take the blame for all of our sins so we could rejoice in an eternity that is free from sin and safe from pain and sorrow. I believe in Jesus. I know His life to be a truth."

The retreat showed me the stairway to climb up and out of this hole is there; it's just not visible yet. But I *will* see it, and I *will* walk up and out. But not alone. God will show me the way in His time, and He will be the one standing right behind me when I can't take another step. I expect I will take two steps up and out of this hole and one step back down over and over and over again. *Exhausting.* I will wait patiently (sometimes impatiently) and hope for a blessing from this tragedy. I know it's coming without any proof that it's out there.

The song "Oceans" by Hillsong spoke to my heart that weekend like never before, yet I'd heard it hundreds of times on the radio. I find I'm barely keeping my eyes above the crashing waves most days, faking it on the phone at work and falling apart the minute the conference call is over. I know some things are coincidence, but I treat little things as signs from Tristan telling me he's right there—the orange folder I got when I checked into the retreat and later found out "all the folders are not orange, Laura" and an orange cross bracelet I randomly received. With the way the bracelets were packaged and handed out to us, there is no way anyone would have known which package I'd get, yet I got one with an orange bracelet! Thanks, buddy. I miss you.

"Oceans (Where Feet May Fail)" by Hillsong United

You call me out upon the waters
The great unknown where feet may fail
And there I find You in the mystery
In oceans deep
My faith will stand

And I will call upon Your name
And keep my eyes above the waves
When oceans rise
My soul will rest in Your embrace
For I am Yours and You are mine

Your grace abounds in deepest waters
Your sovereign hand
Will be my guide
Where feet may fail and fear surrounds me
You've never failed and You won't start now

So I will call upon Your name
And keep my eyes above the waves
When oceans rise
My soul will rest in Your embrace
For I am Yours and You are mine

Spirit lead me where my trust is without borders
Let me walk upon the waters
Wherever You would call me
Take me deeper than my feet could ever wander

And my faith will be made stronger
In the presence of my Savior

Oh, Jesus, you're my God!

I will call upon Your name
Keep my eyes above the waves
My soul will rest in Your embrace
I am Yours and You are mine

What Now?

His room still had the books he was reading on his nightstand until May when I went through all his books and moved most into Colton's closet. There is still laundry in the basket in Tristan's closet, clean clothes hanging along with his #14 basketball jersey he wore the day before his accident at his game. I still tighten and smooth out the comforter if Wyatt sits on his bed to pray. This space once occupied by a living and breathing person is empty. Standing in his room is my only connection, like walking into the past. I so desperately want to snap out of this awful daydream and wake up to realize it's not true. Never happens.

Some of the toys were moved into Colton's room or into a toy closet we keep downstairs. I was always good about rotating to donate toys or move them around. Interesting how toys that have always been there are like new when they haven't been played with in a month or two! I'd clean out a closet, and the boys would be occupied for hours while I sifted through everything. "Hey, I remember that car. Where has this been?"

Some of the clothes that hang in Tristan's closet will eventually go to Colton the way hand-me-downs always made their way into Colton's closet. Some I won't be able to see on Colton. We started to put meaningful mementos into a shoebox, and I typed out a story Tristan had written in a notebook. He loved to write. Other things will be added to the shoebox, and I expect we'll outgrow it and it will eventually be a large bin to fit things like his orange camouflage backpack he carried the last three years (L. L. Bean makes a durable backpack!)—merchandise plug.

There are at least two drawers of trinkets; you know, all that little plastic stuff that ends up accumulating. I'd always go through the boys' rooms about every six months, cleaning out, asking, "Is there a reason why we're saving *this*?" There is a drawer of what I call Tristan's "inventions," things he made from recycled material, blowguns made from empty pen casings, slingshots made with rubber bands, an air blaster made from a water bottle.

At some point, we may move Colton into Tristan's room. It's the bigger of the two rooms upstairs, which would mean changing Colton's room into a second guest room. It seems the logical step, but within the first year, I was not ready and nothing about the idea made sense. Logic got thrown out the window. Packing things up and plucking Colton into this living space seemed like we were removing proof that there was a life occupying this space that is no longer here on earth. I couldn't just do a lift and load. Wyatt was rather adamant about it in the beginning: "His room will not be a shrine." I told him I wasn't ready. This space, this was where I could pretend he was still here, and for some time, I just needed a room I could walk into and be taken back in time for just a moment. Wyatt didn't mention it for a long time, and I think he knew he would miss the space too and the way it made us feel like maybe for one split second this isn't real—he's just at school or at camp or downstairs watching TV.

A large picture of Tristan hangs in the hallway that led to his bedroom. We all pass by it every day. It's a head/shoulders shot of him singing at play practice. I picture he's singing and performing for God's glory now. I hung it so that it's right at his height, the top of his head just gracing the bridge of my nose. The day of his accident, when we walked out of religion class, I had my arm around him and said, "I literally think you've grown two inches since Christmas." I'd say to him in a deep voice, imitating his *future* self, "Hi, Mom. I'm home from school. Could you do my laundry?" and I'd bend my knees to crouch down and look *up* at Tristan, knowing he would soon be taller than me.

I'm only five foot three, so *most* people are taller than me. When he was younger, I would hold him up so he was looking down at me and do the same thing. In recent years, he'd gotten too big to hold up. If anyone was picking anyone up, it was more likely Tristan picking *me* up. He was so strong, so athletic, literally an Abercrombie ad with six-pack abs. People commented on it all the time. "Look at that kid. He's pure muscle." He was lean without an inch of fat on him; built for speed on the football field or basketball court.

I hadn't been to confession in a year. I went a few weeks after Tristan's death, in February and again in March, then May and every two months thereafter. I know this is not a punishment from God, but a clean slate was necessary and I felt a desperate need to be ready for Jesus's return. Processing all of this during the season of Lent felt timely. At a time where Lent is intended to review our life, examine our conscience, and bring us closer to God in preparation for Jesus's death and rising, I was drawing closer to God as I searched for answers, comfort, and peace. I spent time in our adoration chapel and signed up to be a Eucharistic guardian. It's amazing to think there is someone in that chapel 24/7.

I'd always prayed in the morning and evening and sporadically throughout the day if I needed help or wanted to give thanks. My communication with God increased, and I began having more conversations with Him and more time spent in prayer. That's all prayer is really—conversations with God. People who say, "I don't know *how* to pray," can rest assured; there is no right or wrong, although I will say I've learned to pray more *specifically.* Prayer is not just for times we are in despair but in good times too and, as one grows closer to God, in *all* times. The Bible teaches us to give thanks in all circumstances. I began to *thank* God for the trial that had opened my eyes despite the pain.

We view life through a different lens now. First and foremost, our first-world problems we used to complain about seem ridiculous. I used to complain about Wyatt being gone two weeks out of the month, traveling for work while I was "stuck" working full-time and managing the boys solo. So what? I'd give anything to be back to shuffling them from their after-school programs to sports, to race home for dinner, take showers, get to bed. I used to complain about the stress of my job. That was a light cross to carry; the one I have now is more than I can bear. I used to worry about losing Wyatt's dad to cancer. Now I have peace knowing where he is going and am envious he'll see Tristan before I will.

Every day is a struggle. Every hour is a struggle some days. Wyatt and I toggle back and forth holding each other up, talking each other through our dark moments when the tears flow and our selfish thoughts are desperate to get our perfect life back. I so desperately want a vision from God, a booming voice, a sign so clear it could only be His work. *Why do I need this validation?* My faith tells me He hears all my thoughts. He knows my pain. My belief in Jesus and God's grace will grant me a place in heaven where I will spend eternity with God, and I will see Tristan again (along with other loved ones who have gone before me). Again, I hear Him say, "Trust me." *Trust* is mentioned 147 times in the Bible. *Okay, Lord, I hear you.*

A psychologist I saw three times in the first six weeks told me, "Get back to your routine. Get back to work. The sooner the better." I started back part-time at the end of February, only five weeks after the funeral, and full-time the following week, although there wasn't much for me to do. Getting up and out of bed was still a challenge some days, but I tried to be online by nine in the morning. Without enough to do, I'd go to my boss each week to ask for more. I knew he was being gentle and didn't want to overwhelm me, especially since I'd told him I was having trouble focusing for long periods of time. Work was a healthy distraction, but once the distraction was over, reality gives you another gut punch.

Exercise helped. I was an avid exerciser before the accident. I took some time off but got back into it. It does clear my mind, release endorphins, and I'll admit, I'm not as emotional as I can be on the days I don't exercise. By early February, I got back to walking, then running again. By May, the neighbor I was running with got us up to seven miles; way more than the max three miles I'd ever run before. On the days I'd run, we'd head out about 8:15 a.m. and be back by nine thirty. I was back to checking my e-mail after Colton got on the bus and then working about ten to four on average, slowly taking on more each week.

The passion I once had was gone, so I just worked for the distraction and a paycheck. Even the paycheck was less meaningful to me. The title and salary I'd worked so hard for were so unimportant. All I wanted was to get through the day so I could go pick up Colton from school. Days weren't flying by like they used to. Maybe that was a good thing. I'd always wanted to slow down. This was too slow, and my mind would wander. I didn't want to consume my brain with too many distractions as I felt God wanted me in that downtime. I tried to quiet my thoughts to hear Him. My mind, at times, was consumed with the loss, replaying memories over and over. I tried not to relive the accident. The seven days in the hospital is a blur with days and nights blending together.

The first weeks are sad to think about and then we hit one month, two months, three months, and four months. The running and exercise were necessary. I refused to go on antidepressants. I must process the grief; I can't mask it. I counted Sundays adding up the weeks, then months, since the accident. Each week and month that passed, I was still in disbelief. One of these mornings, I was going to wake up and realize it was all a terrible nightmare.

The school was extremely supportive and began working with us on a memorial to Tristan and gathering pictures of him for a tribute page in the yearbook and a fifth-grade farewell slideshow. The Christian program Tristan and Colton attended after school one day a month organized a balloon release (orange balloons, of course). All the while, I'm grateful, but inside, I'm still staying, "What am I doing here?" How am I the mom at the balloon release for *my* son? This can't be real? This is *not* fair.

Tristan was supposed to wow the audience as Captain Hook on February 24. He was going to start taking the bus home from school after the play and mind himself with homework or reading until I was done with work at five. We were supposed to go to Orlando on spring break now that Colton is taller and can ride more rides. We'd go back through all the Harry Potter rides at Universal. Tristan was supposed to have milestone testing in school and pick which foreign language he wanted to take in sixth grade. We were going to rearrange my schedule so I could be there when Tristan got on the later bus for middle school in the fall. *So many plans.* God's word tells me to stop planning and let Him guide my way, day by day.

Our first holiday, Easter, without Tristan, and life felt so sad and empty. My sister and her family and my sister-in-law and her family came to stay with us. Colton was elated to celebrate Easter morning with his cousins (something new), and it helped me too. We mustered through a vacation for spring break (it really wasn't a *vacation*; let's just call it a "trip"). It was hard without a playmate for Colton. After that trip, we said we'd never take another vacation just the three of us.

Mother's Day without Tristan, my favorite holiday, was a sad day. I felt like part of the credential I had been handed for being a mother was stripped away. *Stupid.* I will always be Tristan's mom, but if you've been in my shoes, you know what I mean. Just being Colton's mom wasn't enough. On my very *first* Mother's Day, we sat in the crying room with Tristan at church that morning. Every year, our church hands out a bouquet of flowers to the newest mother and newest grandmother. I won the bouquet of flowers that year for being the newest mother with my precious little four-month-old. Such a wonderful memory.

Later in May, Colton made his First Communion. Flashbacks of Tristan's First Communion were strong. Colton wore the same little navy jacket with the gold button. My mom and Wyatt's aunt and uncle were staying with us, and we had a few friends over after the ceremony. Colton had gone over to a neighbor's to play. I stopped in to bring him home, and another set of neighbors were there having drinks. It was how we used to all hang out, switching who hosted one weekend to the next. They asked me to stay, but I could barely get out the words, "I have to get back." I didn't *need* to get back to family; I had to get out of there. Seeing them, celebrating, I wanted our life back. I barely got down the driveway and was bawling. I went straight to bed without saying goodnight to any of our guests.

How will we get through the summer? We had spent the last three summers up on a lake north of Atlanta. The boys loved tubing and wakeboarding, and Tristan was so good at it. Colton learned to wakeboard when he was six. When I'd had enough of the speedboat, we'd head to our island, the one we'd always stop at, to let the boys play in the sand and throw the football. They loved exploring, and the lake had so many coves and places to stop and find cool rocks and shells. We always came home with a container filled with something from their adventures. How would I host our annual pool party at our neighborhood clubhouse on the last day of school? I was the neighborhood social committee. What about our Fourth of July tradition of going to the parade in the morning and then fireworks that night?

Even traditions as silly as going shopping to stock up on school supplies for the next school year; I loved letting the boys pick out new lunch boxes and folders for the new school year. Then there is every day in between; days that are just as difficult, if not more challenging, than the bigger "milestones." Just going to the grocery store is hard. The boys had come to an age where I could hand them each a few coupons and send them off to the appropriate aisle to meet me back in the produce section. I avoided taking them, but when I did, I gave them responsibilities and would even ask Tristan to compare the price of one *with* the coupon to another *without* to see which would be cheapest. Always a lesson there!

One day, I was in the store and "Crazy Little Thing Called Love" came on, and it felt like Tristan saying, "Hi, Mom. It's me"— an orange moment.

Family had asked us to join them for a vacation in June, but we declined for fear of driving ten hours there and then feeling awful once we got there and not having an "out." His family wouldn't care if we were too upset to stay. They've been amazing. They eventually entertained my wish to do something different for our first Christmas. We've always spent Christmas up north at my in-laws. Walking out to the living room with only Colton is not something

I was willing to do, so we changed it up and my sister-in-law hosted at her house.

We went up to Illinois for the Fourth of July, changing up our routine. I hated it. I'd built these traditions, things we'd done every year of Colton's life, and now I'm changing it for my emotional sanity. Am I depriving him of the whole idea of the consistency of tradition? Does it really matter? Honestly, I don't think Colton thought twice of it; he was elated to spend the Fourth with his cousins and see fireworks.

We fake it as best we can for Colton. He's resilient. He comforts us when he sees us crying. He gives us a hug and tells us "Tristan is in a much better place than here." and I know with conviction that he speaks the truth. I just miss him so much. It's still the first thing we think of when we wake up and the last thing I'm thinking when I go to bed. *Every. Single. Day.*

As we navigate our new path in life, I often think of those who have been in our shoes. We've developed quite the new circle of friends, a group I never wanted to belong to, but they do help us. I often think of Wyatt's grandmother who lost her eighteen-year-old daughter in a boating accident. One of nine children, you think, gosh, she had eight other children, but every parent knows, you could have eighteen children and still feel the loss. If any man has a hundred sheep and one of them has gone astray, does he not leave the ninety-nine on the mountains and go and search for the one that is straying? (Matt. 18:12). From the moment I met his grandmother, I thought, "How did she do it?"

The answer was always "faith." Seven years later, she lost her husband to suicide. Sorrow upon sorrow (Phil. 2:27, NAB). She is now eighty-one, and I wish I could say she received a definitive answer for her trials but I don't think she ever got one. She told us, "The hole in your heart is always there after a loss like this," but over time, she was able to find some joy in her life and it has everything to do with her relationships. Her grandchildren say she's been an inspiration to them, showing them faith can bring you though any trial.

WHAT NOW?

Life is about so much more than our earthly possessions. I've always said, you never see a moving truck behind a hearse. It is about the relationships we have and how we treat others. It's not about what your social media page is showing, what brand of shoes or clothes we're wearing, what kind of bag we're carrying, the car we're driving, or the title on our business card. I'm guilty of it. I know I enjoyed the sense of belonging I felt if I was dressed "in style" or *thought* I was in style? LOL. I don't shop at the mall, so that might be why I struggled from a fashion sense? I pretty much pick up clothes at the same place where I get groceries and toilet paper. Social media has created this world where we compare ourselves to everyone else's highlight reel. Truth is, that's not their truth. Don't ever judge a book by its cover; everyone has a story.

We live in a beautiful house. If you were to judge our book by its cover, you'd see a perfect life with a manicured lawn. We both made good financial decisions after college and worked hard to achieve success within our careers. We bought the cheapest house on the block, and Wyatt put in blood, sweat, and tears over thirteen years to make it what it is today. He won't pay anyone to do what he can do himself and he is handy, so he can pretty much do everything. We didn't overspend to update everything I would have loved to do on day one. Instead, he slowly painted every room, installed crown molding, redid tile floors and fireplace surrounds, backsplashes, you name it. The backyard was his biggest project, encompassing nearly two years to make it the sanctuary it is with a waterfall and stone fireplace. Gold star, Hun. I still love it to this day. There are, of course, things that were on my original wish list that are still on the wish list, but aren't there always projects? We made a commitment long ago that we would pay off our credit card every month and not accumulate debt. We've kept up with that, so some projects just have to wait.

Where Wyatt has a passion for cars, I have a passion for travel. Neither one of us grew up taking regular family vacations, so we made a point to take our kids places and enjoy some adult-only time as well. God-spouse-children-all else. Our adult vacations were a recommitment to putting each other first. We felt if we kept our marriage healthy and strong, it would keep our parenting healthy and strong. Our jobs paid well, and we worked hard to afford these things. Quality time has always been my love language and is even more important to me now. Spending time with Wyatt, Colton, our family, and our friends—that's the good stuff.

All of it is great, but the *one* thing that matters most is our relationship with God and our relationship with others. I've always wanted to just fit in. Now I could care less. God's love for me has *always* been enough. Putting our excess into the house and backyard was because they are where we spent the majority of our time, the four of us. Any vacation we took, it was about spending quality time together, getting away from work to focus on each other. Granted, we could achieve quality time in the car in Atlanta traffic; all else was just an added bonus.

Every once in a while, I'll get this feeling. I'll be doing something mundane at home like rinsing out the coffee carafe or loading the dishwasher, and for just a split second, everything seems normal and then I'll remember. I'll think, "Did I dream it? Am I still dreaming? Maybe I'll snap out of this awful daydream, and I'll be back—back to a regular work day, back to picking them up from daycare at the end of the day." I read a passage in *Jesus Calling*: "The mind is the most restless, unruly part of mankind." Much as we learn to hold our tongue, we must learn to discipline our thoughts. This is the most difficult part of grief. I am not suffering physically. We thank God every day for an abundance of food, warm beds, clothing, clean water, and a roof over our heads. Sometimes I've wished for the physical suffering over this. Take us back, and let us gain this perspective in another way, not like this. Wyatt used to say he could handle anything—anything but the loss of one of his children. This literally was our worst nightmare.

God gave us free will and the ability to think for ourselves because of His abundant love for us. In doing so, we have a choice in our thoughts, words, and actions. Because our suffering is emotional, not physical, we can work to redirect our thoughts away from the accident, away from the if-only and what-ifs. We can reroute our thoughts to Scripture and create a focus on our eternity with God and the unconditional love, belonging, and peace we will feel once we see Jesus face to face and are reunited with Tristan.

After we had Colton, it wasn't long before we made the decision that we were good with two kids. I contemplated a third C-section, and my ob-gyn said she would only do one more. I thought about my career and whether it was worth all the money we would spend in daycare if we had a third. A third child is where I probably would have stayed home. That changed my long-term career path and our financial situation, and we were happy with our two blessings. It's crazy to think I even had those thoughts, reasons why I shouldn't have another child, when all I wanted was to replace my joy and bring another baby into this world when Tristan died. I prayed for twins. Like Job, I wanted God to bless me more than my earlier days. I thought some of my friends having babies in their late thirties and early forties were crazy, especially if there had been a large gap in age from their older ones, but here I was considering it, wanting it. Another friend in my same situation experienced these emotions as do many bereaved parents. You just want to fill the hole in your heart and get that joy back. You can never replace the one you've lost, but when you go from the four of us to the three of us, you want to get back to where you were.

I contemplated the idea with prayer and conversation with Wyatt and a close friend, and about seven months after Tristan died, I told my gynecologist what had happened during my annual visit. Not a normal annual visit with this kind of dialogue. She was in the room with me for what felt like an eternity as I held the "napkin" they give you to wear close to my body. She suggested blood work first to test my AMH hormone. It came back low, and I closed the door on that chapter—or so I thought. I'd been struggling with physical manifestations of the stress at this point, bleeding outside of my cycle, stomach issues, headaches, and so forth. I saw a general practitioner who ran more tests and said, "It's the stress." My sister-in-law was trying hard to get pregnant and suggested I have a few more tests done beyond the AMH test. I spoke to a fertility specialist to have a few more tests done, and Wyatt agreed to entertain the conversation but was not in favor of trying to have another child, although he said he would do whatever I wanted. When you are in this situation, you know how important it is to do anything for your spouse to take away some of the pain they're feeling.

Our consultation with the fertility specialist had me thinking we could do this. He's talking about making this happen, and by this time next year, I'd have a baby? Granted, I'd be forty-six, delivering a baby, but I didn't care. Those hopes of finding happiness in having another baby set us on another emotional roller-coaster ride. Did we really want to have another child in our forties? Did we want to go through the risk of doing this and losing the baby because of my age? Were we willing to take the risk that we could have a child with special needs, after all our family had already been through? Was that fair to Colton?

As we continued to talk to the fertility specialist about IVF, it was clear this was a numbers game and a game I couldn't play. The fertility specialist advised the numbers game gained success in the last seven years as they were able to conduct chromosomal testing on the embryos. An embryo is a fertilized egg. In my mind, that's a life. He presented the scenario that, with drugs, they could increase the number of eggs I'd produce next month, harvest the eggs, fertilize them—say, twenty of them—and then test each one to see which ones were not chromosomally abnormal. I asked, what happens to the embryos that are "abnormal"? Well, they are discarded. Discarded? So because they may have Down syndrome, those embryos are literally being thrown away so the "good" ones go in. I know it makes sense when considering the scientific aspect; no one gets pregnant hoping for a special-needs child or some genetic disorder. The reason women my age miscarry is because of chromosomal abnormalities, but those reside with the egg. I said, "Can't you just test my eggs?" Appears technology isn't here yet for that process.

I was baffled by what doctors were doing and how many embryos were being discarded to get to a good one, but I could empathize with a desperate couple's urgency to do whatever it takes to have a baby. Morally, I couldn't do it. I asked the doctor if they could only harvest and fertilize a *few* eggs and forgo the chromosomal test. They agreed they would, but that didn't change my increased risk of miscarriage and this isn't free. I went ahead with blood work and an ultrasound of my ovaries the next day but knew it wasn't going to work out. Emotional ups and downs, here I was so close to getting what I thought might fill the hole in my heart a little but at a price, and I'm not talking dollars. We could not sacrifice a potential life. Wyatt and I could not take the emotional risk of trying and ending up with nothing, and we couldn't play the numbers game that makes IVF successful so we backed out altogether. I knew God would never be pleased with me if I allowed someone to toss out embryos that had made it through the blastocyst stage long enough to be implanted, abnormal or not.

So the obvious next step is adoption or foster care. Again, we couldn't go there emotionally. I thought, if someone wanted to drop off a perfectly healthy baby at my doorstep, we could guarantee a good life for it, but couples in this situation know that never happens. It's just not that easy. I knew I couldn't go through the pain of foster care, attaching myself emotionally to a child that had to go back. I watched Wyatt's brother and his wife go through that stress. Granted, they ultimately adopted the children, a family of five siblings, but not without stress. We could have handled that kind of stress, but not now, not after going through what we'd just been through, and I couldn't affect Colton like that. We needed to put all of our attention on Colton.

Colton would ask, "Can't we just adopt a seven- year-old?" He desperately wanted to replace the playmate he'd lost and was curious about being an older brother. I told him it was certainly an option for some parents, but we had concerns about dealing with issues that an older child might have. There are parents who can take on those types of challenges; we were just not the right parents for challenges given our situation. After all of that, I closed the door on the topic, although I still prayed God would replace my joy, however He felt that could happen. Wyatt's grandmother had a baby at forty-six;

maybe God would give us a similar miracle? Not likely, but what is a prayer if it's not a lofty expectation that only God can make happen?

I so desperately wanted my perfect life back. There was balance when it was the four of us. I replay this memory over and over again in my head of the four of us climbing into the basket at Six Flags, the one that rides over the whole park like a ski lift giving you an aerial view. I sat on one side with Tristan, and Wyatt sat on the other side with Colton to balance the weight. Locked into that basket with nowhere to go but to sit and enjoy being together as a family. That's what I want back.

Getting There

Those who go through trials and suffering have one of two choices: turn away from God or lean in. I chose the latter. I chose to dive into the Bible, Christian books, videos, and movies documenting lives of the apostles or movies playing out the stories from the Bible or anything to do with an account of heaven. We always have a choice. God gave us free will so we could make our own choices. Every day, I told Tristan, "Make good choices." I still say it to Colton every morning as he gets on the bus for school, and I try to be mindful of my choices in all my thoughts, words, and actions, to put God first. I try to ask myself, "Am I doing this for the glory of God?"

As I draw closer to God, the only analogy that's made sense is one of a doctor who has to perform surgery to "fix" you. He will try to limit the amount of pain placed on you, but he still has to cut into you. He does this for your good, knowing you will recover and be better off than you were, despite the pain. God works within our circumstances much the same. If we were to refuse these trials and tribulations, like a patient refusing surgery to cut out the cancer, wouldn't we be depriving ourselves and acting against our best interests?

We have a choice in everything we do. We have a choice whether we are going to wake up and pray and give thanks for this day. We have a choice to give thanks for our food, hot showers, warm beds, and the love of friends and family. We have a choice in our thoughts and how we judge others. I know I spent a significant part of my life controlling my audible words, but it wasn't until I attended the CRHP retreat that I started to attend to my inner thoughts as well. Just as important! I started to change my judgmental thoughts of others into prayers of gratitude instead of judging. I began to make better choices with my thoughts, words, and actions after Tristan died. I wanted everything I did to be pleasing to God.

Whatever trial we are dealing with, we have a choice. Accepting it's all from the hand of God is a challenge. How could God allow this pain and suffering? I had a hard time with this. I feel like the first few months were this season of doubt and depression and, oh, the questions I posed to God! It's not just my cross I'm carrying; it's the children starving on the other side of the earth. *Why*, God? It's women abused by men; it's temptations that take over and put our life down the wrong path? Why God? Why do you allow cancer and terrible things to happen to good people?

We are in the midst of a battle—a battle of good and evil. God always wins, but He may choose to use our trials to transform and purify us. I relate to the "no pain, no gain" of exercise. We have to tear our muscles for them to grow stronger. God may choose to stretch us to our limits because He knows our faith would grow stronger if we choose to let it. I'm coming around. As I prayed in the hospital for "Thy will to be done," I'm facing the balance of my life with the same surrender. Let me not question, not ask for things to be done as I want them to be but as God wishes. I am the patient, and He is the surgeon. He knows what is best for me, and although I suffer now, He makes no mistakes.

Just a few hours after I typed these words, I read in *Jesus Calling*: "Welcome problems as perspective-lifters." We tend to sleepwalk through our days until we bump into an obstacle that stirs us enough to wake us up. For as much as I prayed and went to church and was living my life as a "good Christian," I was still sleepwalking. This situation has most certainly lifted the veil to allow me to see things differently. This particular *Jesus Calling* passage speaks to me *again* as so many of them do day to day:

> If you encounter a problem with no imme-
> diate solution, your response to that situation
> will take you either up or down. You can lash
> out at the difficulty, resenting it and feeling sorry

for yourself. This will take you down into a pit of self-pity. Alternatively, the problem can be a ladder, enabling you to climb up and see your life from God's perspective. Viewed from above, the obstacle that frustrated you is only a light and momentary trouble. Once your perspective has been heightened, you can look away from the problem altogether. Turn toward Him and see the light of His presence shining up on you.

And sure enough, as this passage speaks to me, the scripture referenced for this day's devotional is Second Corinthians 4:18—the *same* scripture that was on Tristan's HOPE shirt. Of course. it is. Again. I hear, "*trust me.*" Okay, God. It's in your hands now.

At times, I'm strong enough to give thanks to God for this suffering and for the perspective it's given me and how it has drawn me closer to the Word of God. In studying His word, I'm able to witness further to my friends and family and pray differently. Wyatt and I both have a longing for heaven like we never had before, but we do not want to just leave this earth. We'd prefer Jesus come back for *all* His followers. When we say we don't want to be here, it doesn't mean we want to die and leave one or the other alone. Come back for all of us, Lord.

It feels like a double-edged sword sometimes. I want so bad to be in heaven, for my suffering to be over, to be welcomed into God's kingdom where there is no more sorrow, no more tears, and to be reunited with Tristan, but I want to be here for Wyatt and Colton. People who haven't been through this might not understand that. All they see is this life. I had never thought more about the afterlife with the exception of the times Tristan and I spoke of heaven.

Watching the "Imagine Heaven" series hosted by Pastor John Burke at Gateway Bible Church gave me a tremendous amount of peace as he spoke of his research of near-death experiences (NDE's) and the consistency across nearly a thousand accounts he'd read.

It was the first time I had a better visual image—a picture of heaven, of those *in* heaven, living there. It's a real place.

Round and Round

Such dark moments and questions that never end. I call it the merry-go-round. My thoughts go there each time I break down. I am not crazy. I know God can do anything, and so I still pray, "Take me back, back in time, to relive the life I had." I still ask, "How long, Lord? How long before you come back for us so we can all be together again?" I beg, "Wake me up from this nightmare!" I bargain, "Maybe it's just a bad daydream, and I'll snap out of it? Now! Maybe I'll wake up tomorrow, and I'll be up in Wisconsin on our snowmobiling trip New Year's 2016 or getting ready to take Tristan to his birthday party January 14, 2017." And again I plead, "*Why!* Why, why, why, why, why, why? Why didn't you intervene, Lord, and get me up to spare him? Why didn't you intervene in the hospital to save him? How will I live with his pain?" Then I sob, "This can't be my life." I scream, "It's *not fair!*" This merry-go-round happens daily and continued for the first year. Whether I'll ever get off the merry-go-round is still a question.

I don't want to be here. I know Wyatt and Colton need me. Wyatt doesn't want to be here. It's only for Colton. We are imprisoned in our minds, living an empty, lonely life. You can be surrounded by family and friends and still feel completely alone. Our blessings just aren't enough. Either way, I will not give up on God's will. I will never risk my eternity in heaven. In my darkest moments, when I want to push my Bible away and say I'm going to just forget it and walk this life like this is it, I can't. I can't *not* believe. Every time, I question "Is it all true?" the answer is *yes*. I believe God sent His son to prove to unbelievers it is truth. I do believe Jesus died for us; He took one for Team Human and told God we were worth saving. He died so we could be forgiven of our sins. He made such an enormous sacrifice for the human race and lives out an eternity in paradise. I believe this, and I know I will be able to live in that paradise with Tristan one day.

We look at this life on earth through a different lens now. What made us feel complete is gone, and we are broken in pieces on the floor. People who don't understand (which is pretty much everyone) will point out things like living for Colton and living for Wyatt. We *know* our blessings, but they are clouded by the pain. You can't see the good that's right there in front of you when all you can feel is the pain. We don't enjoy the things we used to. People say that will come back in time. Time seems to be the only thing that lessens the pain, but the pain was as strong at one year as it was on day one. If I could just sleep until that time comes, I'd prefer that. You want desperately for the pain to be gone, but at the same time, you *don't* want the pain to be gone because that would mean you've accepted the way things are and living a life that is okay without my son, and it's not.

Every day since Tristan's accident has been a bad day but then there are the really bad days. Wyatt would ask me, "Aside from the obvious, how was your day?" He knew when I said, "Not good," it meant it was a *worse* day. Those days, I spent a lot of time crying, hours crying. Being sad and angry would blend together all the time like stirring milk into coffee. Sadness is there because I can't hear his voice, I can't hug him, and life will never ever be the same. We will never be truly happy again. Anger would stem from people trying to show empathy. Sometimes sympathy is better than empathy.

You don't really know how I feel. Losing your grandparent, parent, or dog is *not* the same thing. Your miscarriage is an awful circumstance but *not* the same thing, and as awful as it is to lose a child to SIDS, I'd still be thinking, "You didn't get to know this child and live with them for eleven years!" Not the same kind of loss. I'd start to cringe when I heard people say "When we lost Dad…" and I'd think, "How long did it take you to get over losing your dad, an individual older than you whom you always knew would go first!" My bereaved moms know what I'm talking about. It's snarky, but someone told me, "We *get* to be a little snarky."

Get better, or get bitter. I refused to become a bitter person despite snarky moments, and that's all they were—moments. I continued to pour my emotions into my journal and writing became part of my therapy.

Five Months

I feel like I've taken three steps backward after I thought I'd taken a step forward. Spending an hour in the chapel every Monday morning for the last month has been peaceful, but I still can't quiet my thoughts. Having friends here for Memorial Day weekend was nice, but they are building their family and ours has fallen apart. It's just hard. Getting away and spending a weekend in LA was just another distraction. Wyatt forgot my birthday was on the Sunday we were flying home. Our brains are mush and I don't want to have a birthday anyway, but it sucks that we would have been celebrating otherwise. Coming home and launching our summer without Tristan has sent me spiraling downward. We still have to get up and work. Thank God we work from home. I would have had so many sick days calling in for headaches and my unwillingness to just get dressed if I had to go into an office every day. I see all these shiny-happy people all the time, and it makes me sick. Wyatt calls it blissful ignorance. They have no idea. It's still amazing to me how the pain can cloud any and all blessings in our lives. I have a great husband, a strong marriage, and an amazing kid, but it's not enough.

I'm up to running seven miles now. It's my therapy, and I'd mentally told myself I could go for ten by end of the summer. Why would anyone *willfully* run ten miles? I cannot believe the words even came about. There are days, like today, my head is pounding from crying last night and again first thing this morning. I'm not running today even though I know it would make me feel better. There is no motivation. Coffee is my only comfort.

I've had thoughts, surely fed by the devil himself. Each time, the battle begins, and I put on my armor and proclaim, "I will never give in and will never give up on my belief in God and His son, sent to be our Savior." I can't help but feel abandoned even when I know I'm not, but I want a sign, a dream, a vision. I want to *know* God hears me still. I want to know Tristan is better. I want to know it won't be long until we're all together again. Wyatt tends to listen to more end-of-times sermons and is sure the end is near. I agree, there is more alignment with John's vision and the book of Revelation than ever before, but I just don't feel like we'd be so lucky. I used to pray to remain healthy so I could raise my boys, and I find myself wanting to be struck with cancer so I can just go. I'm envious of those older and closer to going home even though none of us really knows the date or time, which means age is not always the defining factor of how close we really are. The pain takes over everything, and thoughts can be ridiculous at times.

Six Months

At a time when my whole world was still about my grief, Wyatt's grief, and trying to find our new normal, more sorrow comes upon my family. My dad called three days after Father's Day (June 2017) to tell me they'd made the decision; my stepmom would stop all cancer-fighting drugs and go into hospice care.

My dad and his wife were married in November 1996, a year after my dad had an aortic aneurism and open-heart surgery.

My dad was only forty-nine when one night shoveling show he had shooting pains up his arm and jaw. During his surgery he suffered a stroke while on a heart and lung machine for several hours longer than planned. We were just in disbelief asking, *Would God leave my brother without parents?*

My stepmom had been in the picture years prior, but they'd broken it off and she moved to Texas. I don't remember the first time I met her, but it was some time in 1996 and I think it would have been at my dad's house. I remember my brother's grandparents, who still lived above my dad, were not comfortable with her being there and felt it was too soon. She was good for my dad, good for my brother, and was the glue that held us together.

My sister and I always thought we might have grown apart from our dad if it weren't for her organizing dinners at holidays and the like. She was a great entertainer and had a dish for every occasion. In addition to cooking, she had a creative side and loved scrapbooking. We'd get the most outrageous cards for holidays and birthdays with pictures, and at Christmas, we'd confiscate the bows from her gifts, always decorated with a small flat ornament. Unfortunately, reused bows just never look as good as they do the first time around. When they first married, my sister and I felt a little slighted. The three of them would go off on vacations, vacations we never took growing up, and we felt left out. I didn't harbor the feelings as much as my sister. I've always just accepted the relationship we have with our dad, but my sister always wanted so much more and time and time again was disappointed when it didn't work out that way.

My stepmom was diagnosed with breast cancer in November 2013. My sister and I had just been through the journey of breast cancer survival with our mom. Upsetting news of my mom's cancer turned into faith-filled hope, and chemo, radiation, and surgery healed her. With an answered prayer, we felt our stepmom's diagnosis was not a death sentence, just another obstacle in life. Her type of breast cancer quickly led doctors to keep looking, and they found cancer in her bones. Still, we held onto hope and knew with treatment, some patients live with bone cancer for ten years! *What doesn't kill you makes you stronger.* The treatment was harsh on her body and she suffered more from the chemo than the cancer, but it was somewhat stable until they found it in her lymph nodes. Ultimately, the lymph nodes were draining into her lungs, and she spent much of June 2017 in the ER to have her lungs drained. Catheters were put into her lungs, so my dad could drain them from home. She lived another three weeks after she decided to bring hospice care into their home.

My dad called on June 21, and on June 25, I was on a flight up to Illinois. I'd planned to drive up to Illinois with Wyatt and Colton on July 1 for a week's vacation and then meetings in Chicago, so I just went a week early. I hadn't been in my dad's house in almost ten years. They had two German shepherds, and I was terrified of the dogs. But mostly it was because my sister's house was "base camp" and where we always stayed when we were up north, so my dad and stepmom often came to see us there.

Needless to say, the dogs had destroyed their carpet, there was dog hair everywhere, and the house was in desperate need of purging and cleaning. I'm a dog lover (except for German shepherds) but I'm also a neat freak, so we don't have pets in our house. I did have a cat once—cat hair everywhere. *I digress.* My stepmom's brothers and sisters-in-law met me at the house and helped with "operation clean out." Two and a half days after we'd been there, I was allowed upstairs (after most of the piles of clothes, bags, and so forth had been cleared). I spent hours continuing to clean and organize and kept thinking, "God has called me here to do what I do best." I'm *always* cleaning and organizing, so who better to do this and provide my stepmom with the peace of mind that this was *done*? No burden on my dad when she passes; it would all be taken care of.

We donated several car loads, and little by little, order from chaos. Two weeks later, I left to visit Wyatt's family, our first Fourth of July without Tristan. We'd confirmed we couldn't do our traditional drive down to the parade and fireworks that evening—too many painful memories. Wyatt and Colton drove up to my in-laws in Central Illinois, and I drove down from Chicago. That weekend, we released sky lanterns in honor of Tristan, a great idea my sister-in-law thought of, and she ordered enough for all the aunts, uncles, cousins, and grandparents to participate. As the lanterns lifted up over the cornfield, they turned into orange balls of light. Orange. Tristan was surely smiling.

It was difficult to watch Colton do sparklers without his brother. I could see how everyone's lives just kept moving along despite how ours felt stuck in anguish and pain. I just wanted to go home, but we'd committed to spending a few days with my sister and nephews and planned a day at Six Flags on the Friday after the Fourth. Colton loved it and loved being with his cousins going on roller coasters. Wyatt and I were crippled inside, remembering such good times when we'd gone to Six Flags over GA with Tristan and Colton in October 2016 and bought season passes to go back the summer of 2017. *Our plans, not His.*

When you lose someone, the pain isn't coming from the things *they* won't get to do. Tristan is in heaven. If he wants to ride a roller coaster, he can. God's kingdom offers all the joy and thrills we have here on earth, times one thousand! The pain is trying to continue doing the things Tristan loved, things Colton loves, without our precious son. Tristan brought such laughter and joy into our lives, and to not have that is why I still cry, every single day for six months.

My stepmom passed away the morning of July 9, 2017. Both of my dad's wives passed in July. Perhaps God didn't want my dad to have *another* month with painful memories; just keep it consolidated to July? We all helped my dad plan the funeral, and I put together poster boards with pictures we went through. I channeled my stepmom's scrapbooking abilities for the poster boards. *Two funerals in six months.* A few days before her service, I was on the funeral home's website, and the latest obituary was displayed on the home page. The name was familiar, and the boy was only nineteen. I thought, "No, please, God, no." Sure enough, it was a friend's son—a man I've kept in touch with for twenty-two years, having worked in the same office together in the midnineties. He had lost his son suddenly to a health-related issue with no signs or symptoms. I contacted him immediately to express my condolences. I was able to give him and his wife a hug just before *our* formal service began.

Although I was in so much of my own pain, I felt called to do anything I could do to help and offered my phone number and e-mail address. I had so little time, all I could tell them was "I'm still standing." I told them "my faith is why" and repeated what I've said so many times in the last six months: "When this happens, you have two choices: you can turn away from God or lean in. We are still standing because we lean in."

Seven Months

It's amazing to me how many people have *not* reached out and asked me how I'm doing. Was I one of those people to someone else who was expecting me to check in during a bad time in their life? I can guarantee I was at *some* point. I ask God for forgiveness for those times. Silly that I've asked and been forgiven *already*, so why bring it up to God again? I guess that's human; sometimes we can't let go of shame or guilt. I've thought about how I might redo life, but I'd never want to do a thing differently if it meant I wouldn't end up with Wyatt and my two boys. I still ask God to take me back. He's God, He can do *anything*, and so you may think it's an *unrealistic* request, but I don't. I want to go back to November or December 2016 or to that afternoon in January. I want to prevent the accident from taking my son, but I ask God to leave me with this perspective I have. I never want to go back to how I saw things before. It's like the guy in *The Matrix* who asks to go back in, and he doesn't want to remember that the real world is what it is. Ignorance is bliss. I want this perspective, this longing for heaven, this relationship with God, this ability to witness, but I want my son back.

On August 13, 2017, we held a bake sale for Tristan with all proceeds going to his memorial fund and WinShape Camps. A neighbor I didn't know well prior to Tristan's accident was affiliated with Little Helpers of Atlanta and asked months prior if they could do something for Tristan. They came up with "Baking It Forward" to align with our Pay It Forward cards, and many people contributed baked goods, cookies, cakes, bars, brownies, you name it. Some of the bakers were strangers to me, and I was so very grateful for their generosity. We grossed $5,300 in just a few hours. *Unbelievable.*

Wyatt didn't care to stand and say hello to all those who came by to make purchases/donations and opted to stay down by our pool while I did what I could to hold it all together and say hello and thank you to hundreds of people who came to support us. The room was decorated in orange. All the baked goods were individually wrapped and had an orange heart with a motivational saying or scripture. I loved keeping Tristan's spirit alive with an event like that. You want to scream out, "Don't forget him, *ever*," because I know people's lives go back to the way they were. Complacency sets in, and people are back to being consumed with work or the kids' schedule or the next home-remodeling project. Life stands still for us, and every single day, I shake my head and ask God to let me wake up. This isn't my life; this can't be my life.

Seven and a Half Months

Over these last several months, I've met with a St. Stephen's minister from my church. She has listened to me as I've circled round and round the same feelings and emotions each week. Each week, she listens, then she prays over me. She continues to pray for me when we're not together, which is a great comfort to me. I'd spoken to her about my silent retreat at the Ignatius House in Atlanta to focus on mindfulness and stress relief. We learned about breathing, and I found clarity accessible in just a few deep breaths. The mind is responsible for much of the stress on our bodies, so we learned to use our minds to do the opposite of stress and calm our minds, even begin to heal them. For the record, a bereaved parent never heals. I will never be the same again, and the hole that's left me feeling so very empty inside will never close completely.

The weekend was a mix of men and women of Christian and Jewish faiths and those without; it was a blend of all walks of life and career affiliations. I had never attempted meditation, so this was new territory for me. I enjoyed the silence, particularly when I didn't feel obliged to make small talk. I took advantage of quiet moments to pray and walk and just be still. We learned a lot about breathing and practiced guided meditation and yoga. *Mindfulness* was not a word I'd used in my vocabulary prior, so I was enlightened by a community of experts in mindfulness. My body was showing physical signs of the stress, and I was open to finding a way to relax without antidepressants that some people tend to push as if it's the only solution. Why is it acceptable to take a pill you know nothing about (or its side effects) but it's not enough to combat depression with exercise, friends, prayer, and meditation? I don't get it. People just can't accept that being sad for however long the season of grief lasts is *okay*. My son died, I'm going to be sad for a *long* time, so just get used to it!

Toward the end of the retreat, we had a meditation that included imagery. We were standing on the bank of a river. The river represented our thought process, and just like boats come down the river, some fast, some slow, those thoughts flow into our consciousness and back out. We can keep some of those thoughts around a long time, or we can let them pass through. The exercise was about recognizing the thought and letting it be just that, a thought, then calmly letting it pass.

I attached my thoughts to different vessels. Here comes the rickety Tom-Sawyer-looking raft, representing harsh words, judging me without realizing each time shards of wood are left floating in my river. Then there is the canoe teetering to the left then to the right until it topples over with all of its emotions spilling into my river; emotions I don't have the strength to console. Next is the submarine that approaches quietly then springs up out of the water disrupting any sense of calm, making waves, and affecting all other boats. Last was a large barge. This one wasn't passing through; it was tethered to the side, anchored for a while. How long would it be here? The outside was filthy. It would require a *lot* of work before it was in shape to float down the river again. Some damage could never be repaired; maybe patched up but never really the same. Each vessel was an obvious representation of emotions and people in my life. Some days, I just want to scream, "Get out of my river!"

With sadness and grief come so many other emotions I needed to define for my mental clarity: anger, bitterness, jealousy.

What am I angry about? I'm angry people are afraid to call or text me to ask how I'm doing. You're afraid? Of what? If I don't want to pick up the phone or text back, I won't, but to ignore me is just hurtful. I'm angry they've all gone back to their lives as if it didn't happen, as if I'm not *dying* inside. Yes, please, tell me again how you were out celebrating while I can't stop crying every day. Maybe I've teetered into bitterness. *What is the difference between being angry and bitter?*

I guess anger comes first and is tied to the moment where bitterness rears its ugly head when you haven't let go of the anger. And I assume it's caused by the jealousy. I feel jealous I don't have joy in my life that came from Tristan's presence, his humor and wittiness, his athleticism, his thoughtful nature. I am jealous of the future you all still have with your kids; a future I've lost. People say, "But you still have Colton." Do you really think having half of what I had before even comes close to making it okay? If you lost both your arms, and I said "But you still have your legs," does that even make sense? No. The anger, bitterness, and jealousy weren't even a boat in my river; it was the scum and slime that collects and ends up floating along the bank of the river with some empty bottle or cigarette butt that got tossed in. *Sludge.*

Shortly after the retreat, I heard back from one of the organ recipients, the sixty-seven-year-old grandmother who received Tristan's lungs. Speaking of anger, at first, I was angry his lungs went to someone who may not be on the earth a very long time, but I realize she has a family who loves her. It's not fair I have to live without my eleven-year-old son while an old lady gets to live out her retirement watching grandchildren I may never have. The retirement I used to look forward to is filled with anxiety now. What will Wyatt and I do when Colton leaves us to go to college or just move out? What if Colton can't have kids? What if we are stuck here for twenty more years and couldn't even have grandchildren?

How could God allow this tragedy, and if it will reveal a blessing or His glory, when will we see it? If never, I just want out of this prison sentence. He's left me in. We are held behind bars without a way out of our pain. It's cold and empty, and I'd just rather Jesus came for me now. Untie the barge, and let me float out to sea.

Eight Months

They say not to make any rash decisions for the first year: don't move, don't change careers, don't run out and have a baby, no major purchases you'd regret. One year is the "norm" because that must be how long it takes before you're in your right mind again. My friend who lost her son in February 2015 still cries when we get together and talk about our situations. She's the one who backs me up when I tell her what gets under my skin because she gets it 100 percent. She understands the anger. She knows I'm not a mean person; it's just an emotion that comes and goes. Some natural disaster would be on the news and it would be awful to see people had lost their homes, but both of us would be like, "Boohoo, you'll recover. We lost our *sons!*" We're angry it happened to us and not someone else even though we'd never wish this pain and suffering on our worst enemy. We're not mean people insensitive to the idea of another's difficult circum-stances; it's just about how we feel in a moment. We'd give anything to have lost our homes, our jobs, or our arms and legs if it meant we could have our sons back.

I can't even truly describe the pain and emptiness. It's a hollow feeling and a despair like no other, knowing I have to finish this life without Tristan in it. I've said it before; it's like being put into prison for something you didn't do. Ever see the movie *The Shawshank Redemption* where he not only loses his wife but is also put behind bars for *years* for a murder he didn't commit? Yes, he crawls through a tunnel of slop and escapes to Mexico in the end, but he lost his wife and he lost *years* of his life in the clink. Mexico is great and he finds joy again because he's no longer imprisoned. We feel like we will always be behind these bars, shackled with grief. I can relate to how desperate he was; so desperate he'd climb through the sewer. I've had so many emotional days I felt like I'd just climbed through the sewer. It's ugly, it's exhausting. I didn't end up on the beach in Mexico though.

I've read that in order to be transformed, I have to shed my former self like a snake sheds its skin. *Is it God who wants to transform me? Couldn't there have been another way? Was I so far from being the person God wanted me to be that I've had to endure this kind of suffering to prove my faith? Why did God allow Job to be tested the way he was?* Sometimes I feel like a pawn in a spiritual warfare between God and Satan.

When I look back over the first several months, it's as if it's a dream I sort of remember. January 2017 is a blur, but I have precious memories of dancing with Tristan on New Year's Eve and riding down to Milwaukee back to the airport on New Year's Day to fly home after two weeks away. The boys played with their new robots and tried to mysteriously place a robot under someone's seat at the airport and make a funny noise. Tristan called Grandpa using a pay phone that was still at the airport. We celebrated his eleventh birthday with a steak dinner I made and brownies for dessert on January 3. His birthday party at the rock climbing place seems surreal, and our last day with Tristan, January 15, was like any other Sunday.

February, we were still home full-time on bereavement leave. I don't even know what we did with our days except sleep half the day after getting Colton off to school. Our first trip out in public to Target to get Colton his valentines was a challenge for us. We ran into two to three people we knew, and they were all standing around us like a celebrity who gets stopped by paparazzi. Eventually, Wyatt had that look like "Get me the heck out of here," so my friend grabbed the valentines and said she'd pay for them and drop them at our house. Abort mission! Abort mission! We went home empty-handed.

I'd been helping out one day a week after school for the play so it was a distraction for me and something I could do with Colton, but every time I was in the gym rehearsing with the boys, I would wait for Tristan to just come walking through the doors. Tristan was one of the leads in the play for the second year in a row, and someone else had to take his place. The knife just dug deeper every time

I thought about it. The school play the year prior was my proudest moment of Tristan. I could not believe his ability to be on stage, in character, delivering his lines in an English accent without missing a beat. He was funny, and he could sing! He was amazing. Losing him felt like God was stripping me of my pride, like a zip-up suit I had to peel off and step out of and walk away from. Being out in public was the first step in trying to be normal again.

We took Colton to the Ringling Bros. Circus mid-February to try to do something fun for him. Tristan would have loved it. Everything we did brought about thoughts of what we no longer had with Tristan gone. Colton started spring baseball, and we were set for another distraction. Wyatt's birthday was grazed over, and we were both back to work in March. Wyatt re-acclimated to work, and I felt like I was starting a new job. Granted it was a new role, but my boss sheltered me, a little too much at times. However, I was back to full-time later that month. My company was great about being flexible with me. Each week, I'd ask for a little more until I was at a point where I could get enough done with the limited attention span I still struggled with.

We took a weekend and drove down to St. Petersburg, Florida, March 11 to 12 for a race. Our situation was like a low-hanging cloud that followed us around even though it was a beautiful weekend weather-wise. Spring break felt like a mistake, trying to do something just the three of us, but we went to Myrtle Beach for a few days. It is possible to be on a beautiful beach *and* be miserable. My sister, brother-in-law, and nephews came for Easter but spent as much time in the car getting here as they did actually being here. I was happy to have my nephews there; otherwise, there would have only been one Easter basket that morning.

Colton made his First Communion mid-May, and it was a special day for him. I cried through the prayer all the parents had to read to the communicants. His First Communion workshop was held the Saturday after Tristan's funeral. I do not know how I made it through being at church for three hours, but I did it. I can't even imagine what I looked like. We had a small get-together at the house after Colton's First Communion, but my thoughts kept diverting to how we had been celebrating Tristan's First Communion just three years ago. And that's pretty much how every single day was, constantly reflecting back. Wyatt's aunt and uncle and my mom were here, which helped provide a distraction, but I was overcome that Saturday evening and snuck up to my bedroom and went to bed.

We went up north at the end of May for my niece's baptism and then Colton finished second grade. I don't know what I said to people at the end-of-school party I'd planned as I kept up my duties as social chairperson for the neighborhood HOA. *Distraction.*

At the beginning of June, we went to Los Angeles for a company retirement party Wyatt had to speak at. Minutes before he was to get up on stage and introduce speakers, a friend and coworker of his started choking. Wyatt saw his wife's face and ran over. She was beginning to panic and knew she was too small to Heimlich him herself. Wyatt saw his friend holding up a finger like, "Hang on, I got it," and then he was changing color.

Wyatt gave him a warning and said, "I'm gonna go. I'm going," and started the Heimlich on him until a piece of meat came out, freeing his airway again.

Wyatt said it must have taken about ten to fifteen pumps. He came back to the table, sweating a little and shaking. My initial response was, "You're going to be great tonight," thinking he had reservations about being the emcee for the evening. Then he told me what happened; CPR on his son and now the Heimlich on his friend in the span of six months? *My poor husband, he needed a break.* He got up on stage just minutes after and spoke as eloquently as if it hadn't happened at all. He's amazing. Emotions and thoughts came up later, as expected. Why was he able to save his friend but not Tristan? What is going on God?

Later that June, two of my girlfriends from the neighborhood took me downtown the weekend after my birthday to have dinner, stay overnight, and have facials the next morning. It was a nice night out, but I was anxious to get home the next day. Another friend visited the following weekend. It was distraction after distraction, and I just tried to keep the calendar filled.

After spending the end of June and first part of July up in Illinois helping my Dad, I was a wreck. My body was saying, *"Slow down, and take a break already."* We kept a trip we'd planned and went to Hilton Head Island with my sister-in-law, her husband, and my nephew at the end of July for some relaxing beach time. The following weekend, Colton started football conditioning and then we started school August 10. The bake sale for Tristan was August 13, then we went to Chattanooga for a weekend to watch the eclipse in the *path of totality* in some small town in Tennessee. We just kept busy, and at night, I felt I needed to listen to a sermon. I couldn't fall asleep without headphones in my ears with someone preaching. I was avoiding the quiet time.

Following the mindfulness retreat August 25 to 27 and a lot of bouncing around, I finally saw a new general practitioner August 30 and bawled my eyes out in his office explaining my situation and the physical manifestation of my stress. I refused antidepressants, agreed to some tests, and ultimately there was nothing wrong with me. Final answer: *healthy as a horse*; it was the stress. We went up to stay the night at a friend's lake house for Labor Day—the friend I'd been running with. This was good downtime, but we were only comfortable staying one night and headed back home the next day.

Bah Humbug

Ten months out, and another holiday (Thanksgiving) under our belt. It wasn't getting any better. The pain was just as strong as it was on day one, so the fact that we were approaching the one year anniversary of his death meant nothing. When I'd get inside my head, I'd think, people expect us to be different when it's been a year. *Or do they?* Are they watching us as closely as I think they are? *Probably not.* Most are more oblivious and consumed with their own lives, not ours. Thanksgiving was a challenge with an empty seat at the table. The emptiness fills up and spills over into every crevice of my body. In ten months, I only recalled *one* day I didn't cry hard. One day in ten months. I continue to say "This can't be my life" every single day.

I do my best to keep up for Colton so his home life remains as close to what we had before. However, I didn't get a pumpkin at Halloween. That meant we didn't carve pumpkins. I didn't roast and salt the seeds after an hour of sifting out "goop." He never said anything, so I don't think it left some kind of lasting scar. I'll take the pass and try to do better next year. I thought I put enough effort into having the Halloween party at the neighborhood clubhouse and Wyatt put in many hours to help with his costume, so we didn't check out completely.

We changed things up at Thanksgiving, and we did not go visit Santa with my nephews like we've done every year for several years. Wyatt couldn't do his traditional blessing before we ate. We had the kids write down what they were thankful for on the placemats, and I had them decorate the handprint turkeys they drew so Wyatt was off the hook. When I had my moments, I'd go upstairs. I don't know why, but I don't let go of my emotions easily in front of people.

As I stuffed the bird, I thought this is what I've been doing for ten months, stuffing my emotions until the time was right for me to let it all out.

Of course, once the pop-up timer on the turkey was done, people were putting up their trees and lights for Christmas. There was one house down the street that still had a pumpkin out next to the Christmas lights. C'mon, pick a holiday. Personally, I have an aversion to putting up decorations too soon. My benchmark is it has to be within the month the holiday is occurring. This means no pumpkins out in September; Halloween is in October. No lights or trees at Thanksgiving; Christmas is in December.

Then there are the TV commercials preparing for Christmas. I told a friend it wanted to make me puke! Enough already; maybe some of us do *not* think it's the most wonderful time of year. My favorite Christian radio station starting playing Christmas music the day after Thanksgiving. *Really?* Did they do this *last* year? I told myself I'm not doing Christmas cards; I mean, what would I write? *Bah humbug, hope you have a Merry Christmas because our lives* suck. I'll refrain from sending that one out. I nixed a few gifts. I had no desire to shop for anything, and frankly, I didn't want to buy a gift, wrap a gift, give a gift, or get a gift. I wanted to crawl into a hole for all of December and January.

We declined holiday party invitations. We were not in the mood and did not have the capacity to laugh or sing or joke around. There were so many emotions swirling around in my head based on scenarios I've played out that may or may not occur over the holidays. I told myself to go back and reread scripture about not planning and worrying. There were visits with people we hadn't seen in months that I just didn't want to have. There was family who had been absent the last ten months, so what would I say to them? Normally, we'd be catching up on 2017 and recapping funny stories and talking about plans for 2018. *Nope, not doing it.* The only party I wanted to go to was the Bah Humbug pity party.

Then there were the Christmas cards. Normally, I'd enjoy getting cards as much as I enjoyed putting our annual card together.

Not the case this year. Only two cards had a heartfelt handwritten note that called out how difficult this first Christmas would be for us. All the other cards were cheery pictures similar to the life we *used* to have. All I saw was "Here is a picture of our perfect family even though your family has fallen apart this year. Merry Christmas, and Happy New Year anyway!" Sorry, it's raw emotion here, and that's how it felt. Ah, here's that perspective I keep referring to… Was I ever insensitive to someone who was going through a rough time and I sent them my cheerful Christmas card without handwriting, "We are praying for you" or Thinking of you"? I'm so sorry for the times I was oblivious to another's emotions. The holidays are not joyful for everyone. I get that now.

Instead of crawling into the hole I wanted to spend all of December and January in, we went up to Illinois and Wisconsin for Christmas. Spending eleven days sleeping in seven different places is not ideal, and I hated most of it. I just wanted to go home, but I was there to make Christmas as normal for Colton as it could be. About the time we were as far north as we were going to go and it was -15 degrees out, I told Wyatt I'd rather be having a root canal! I was able to squeeze in a little exercise when we stayed at hotels and brought my pillow from home for comfort, but my back was always killing me after sleeping in different beds.

I still kept thinking, "This is not my life. This can't be real." Last New Year's Eve, I slow-danced with Tristan, and I remember thinking what it would be like to dance with him at his wedding. Bah humbug.

Anchor of Hope

By month eleven. I'd adjusted to the holiday stuff a bit. It was still in my face on television, at every store, and is the first thing everyone asks about, but I did get some decorations out after Colton asked if we were putting up a tree. We'd skipped a few parties but managed to get a little shopping done and obligatory gifts wrapped. I was still crying every day, but there were still some days where it was nearly unbearable. I hate those days. I manage it with prayer and exercise as best I can. When it's really bad and I can't even get it together to exercise, I end up sitting on my couch in my pj's, drinking coffee.

Atlanta got hit with a snowstorm before Christmas, and I had no idea how the snow would trigger emotions and memories of our last few weeks with Tristan—our last Christmas together, our last snowmobiling trip, and a week before Tristan's accident, we had our annual snowfall and Tristan played outside in the snow. Watching all the kids come out to play in the snow without him was so difficult. I'd let my mind play a trick on me, and I'd look out the window and think, "There he is. He's going to turn around, and that's going to be Tristan. This will all be a bad daydream—a terrible nightmare." Then the kid turns around, and although he is Tristan's height with dark hair, it's just our neighbor. I think, "Why did this have to happen to us?" I selfishly ask why this had to happen to *my* son. Colton didn't have his brother to play with this time. I hated it. I hate watching him go outside to play in the snow and knowing he has to rely on neighbor kids to play with. I hate that he has to grow up without his older brother. *This life is not fair.* I would have taken any pain God wanted *me* to go through, but why Colton? Why does this poor little boy need to suffer this kind of loneliness? I hate it. *I don't want this.*

Mid-December, I attended a reunion for the November retreat I did, and it was a faith-filled day. The kind that turns up the volume on *hope* and gives the reminder someone in my shoes needs. Hope is *not* lost. *I* am *going to build a ministry by paying it forward.* I spoke for a few minutes about why I'd originally attended the retreat and what I got out of it. I talked about my orange moments and spoke to the perspective, strength, and hope I felt during the retreat and after the weekend came to an end. I committed to serve on the next retreat and attend a weekly Bible study. It's no coincidence the theme of the next retreat is "Anchor of HOPE."

I had another orange moment that afternoon at the reunion that brought me to tears. Just that morning, I'd told everyone an orange moment was something presented to me without explanation that assured me Tristan was not far. We played a game where everyone starts with a present and a story is read. Every time the word *left* or *right* is used in the story, you pass the present to the left or right. Well, let me tell you, ten or so presents passed through my hands back and forth and back again. At one time or another, I was doubled up with presents in both hands, trying to figure out which one to hand which way. When I opened the gift, I was left holding at the end of the game, it was orange candies. *Orange.* A few of the women looked at me like "you've got to me kidding me!" *Divine intervention.* No other explanation as far, as I'm concerned. I'm so thankful for these little signs.

Looking back on the year, I would be remiss if I didn't summarize what I did in our situation to foster *hope* for this reality we are living now, and being that I'm a project manager, I feel for those of you who so desperately want a checklist. I am not a doctor or a licensed practitioner; this is just what I found helped me.

1. Faith: I mentioned before, if you do not have a faith foundation, it's not a matter of *if*—it's *when* you have to deal with something big. Maybe it won't be a cross as heavy as mine, but if it is, the hope that faith provides is lifesaving.

My faith assures me I will see my son again in an eternity that will be so much better than this fallen world.

2. Exercise: Sixty minutes three to six times a week; endorphins *do* help.

3. Sleep: Exercising facilitates better sleep; being sleep-deprived made my emotions worse. At times, I would take one to three milligrams of melatonin to help fall asleep when my brain wouldn't shut down. Reading or listening to sermons was my other go-to.

4. Avoid or limit alcohol: Alcohol is a depressant, and although everyone associates winding down with a glass of wine, alcohol can make the emotions worse.

5. Support: I mixed it up with a St. Stephen's minister from our church; a workout buddy and good friend, new friends who had been in the same situation, meeting old friends for coffee, breakfast, or lunch, and joined a ministry to help serve other women who help me as much as I help them.

6. Take the pass: I took a much-deserved pass on many occasions by declining invitations, skipping certain events, and avoiding certain situations or conversations. I also said yes to offers to bring dinner at the beginning and at the one-year anniversary.

7. Relief: At times, it was a massage or just the quiet time I spent in church, reading scripture or praying, other times a walk or a long bath, but I did my best to get away from it all and take care of myself. The retreats I attended were beneficial for me and a relief for my soul. Even if I had to hide away, crying was relief.

8. Pay it forward: Doing something for others on Tristan's behalf made me feel good knowing I was getting his name out there and making someone else's day a little better.

I made it through the month of January 2018, but not without going on yet another roller-coaster ride with my emotions. His birthday, the accident, his death, the organ donation surgery—all these anniversaries in the month of January. My neighbor rustled up a few others to bring us a week's worth of meals, which actually lasted two weeks. Lasagnas and stews, casseroles and enchiladas, chicken parmesan, chili, all different combinations of salad, cookies, brownies, and even brownies with cookies baked *into* them (brookies). I think I gained five pounds that week.

I had a day I couldn't hold it together, couldn't stop crying, and a day of anger, more crying, on top of the bit of crying I had done every day for 365 days. I'm still sad and mad and all things in between. A year means nothing; the pain is still as bad as it was day ne. I'm emotionally exhausted and still searching for distractions. Even on a day when I'm really mad and I want to push my Bible away and say forget it, all of it, I can't. I can't *not* believe. I know there is a reason God allowed this. I know He has a purpose for the pain. I can't shake the feeling there is something so much bigger going on here. I often role-play my conversation with Jesus when I get to Heaven, nodding my head as He begins to explain why it had to be this way, thanking me for not turning away, for leaning in, for trusting, for enduring and then he'll show me the ripple effect our lives had on others.

I still don't know His plan, but I've grown closer to God as a result of this experience. I will practice letting go of my need for a plan, my need for a checklist, and my need for God's validation where He can say, "Good job, Laura. You're 40 percent of the way through this trial. Keep on walking." *Doesn't work like that.*

Walking by faith means trusting when all else says otherwise, so *here I am, Lord.* Let my message be heard. Let my story help at least *one* person out there. From my broken heart to yours, lean in, trust in God, pay it forward and savor your orange moments.

Tristan singing in drama club practice.

Rock climbing for his eleventh birthday
party the night before his accident.

Tristan in pre-school and 11 years old.

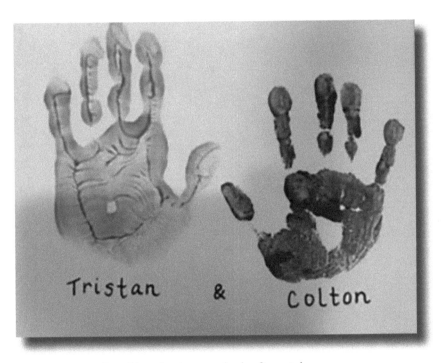

Boys' hand prints made the first night we
were in the hospital Jan 15, 2017

Tristan Dec 2016 in his infamous HOPE shirt

Me with Tristan as Scar in the Lion King Feb 2016

Tristan as Scar in the Lion King Feb 2016

An answered prayer, my heart-shaped stone
found on Myrtle Beach April 2017

Tristan & Colton Dec 2016

Family at Colton's 8th bday party, Tristan in his HOPE shirt

Tristan October 2016

That look. "Let me think about that". Taken at school (5th grade)

Football #25, Basketball #14. Our license plates now say TPS 14

PAY IT FORWARD

Use this card to tell your drive-thru
cashier that you would like to pay
for the person behind you :)

In Loving Memory of
Tristan Schupbach
1/3/06 - 1/19/17

Ask the cashier to give them
this card in order to continue to...
Pay it Forward !

Pay It Forward

"Let us not grow tired of doing good,
for in due time we shall reap our harvest,
if we do not give up."
Galatians 6:9

About the Author

Laura is a faith-filled wife and mother living in the Atlanta area. She has a twenty-plus-year career in project management and enjoys teaching children's liturgy at church, volunteering with local ministries, exercising for mental clarity, and drinking strong coffee. Laura and her husband founded the Tristan Schupbach Memorial Fund, supporting WinShape Camps and other endeavors to foster a child's relationship with God. Laura is passionate about inspiring others through Scripture and launched OrangeMoments.org to continue to spread hope through her writing.